"*I knelt in the center of the room, resting my elbows on a wooden chair. The bare light above me gave the room a clinical look and I closed my eyes to shut it out. I felt very alone and wondered why my wife and I had to go through this time of confusion. 'What are You doing with us, Lord?' I cried. The words had no sooner left my mouth when I became conscious of being surrounded. If someone were to relate to me this incident which I am describing, I would ask a multitude of questions. As a matter of fact, I did ask many that night. Who were these magnificent beings? Were they real or imaginary? Why had they come—to me?*"

# ANGELS

## HOPE PRICE

AVON BOOKS ◆ NEW YORK

The extracts from the Winter 1982 edition of *This England* magazine are reproduced by permission from *This England* magazine, Cheltenham.

The extract from *The Unseen World of Angels and Demons*, Bisilea Schlink, is quoted by kind permission of Evangelische Marienschwestern-schaft.

AVON BOOKS
A division of
The Hearst Corporation
1350 Avenue of the Americas
New York, New York 10019

*To Geoff, Luke and Naomi*
*for never failing to love and support me*

# CONTENTS

# ACKNOWLEDGMENTS

My thanks go to all the friends and family, especially the church family of Hampreston and Stapehill, for praying for us during the two years the book has taken to research and write. Their encouragement and prayers have been invaluable.

Many people have also helped in material ways. Tricia Harrison, Nigel Large and David Harlow have lent me word processors for months at a time. My husband, Geoff, my father, Dick Marshall, Clare Moss, Anthony Grey, and Richard Green have helped with the research. My whole family have helped in very many ways to enable me to complete this book.

# FOREWORD
### BY
# DAVID SUCHET

This century has often been deemed to be the century of the greatest advancements. Certainly mankind is living in an extraordinary world. Imagine what an Elizabethan might make of these commonplace objects: cars, telephones, calculators, fax machines, televisions, movies, airplanes, not to mention spacecraft!

When we read the Bible, we learn about how people lived over two thousand years ago. We also read frequently about how angels appeared to many individuals. Do we ever expect to see angels today? I think, for the majority, the answer would be "No." Let me confess, *my* answer would have been "No"—and how wrong my thinking would have been.

Hope Price felt herself called to write a book about angels, and in so doing proves their existence, not only in Biblical times, but during this century also.

Men and women from all walks of life have shared
their experiences, which changed their way of thinking forever. They were not the product of an over-
vivid imagination or wishful thinking. Such statements
as "The power and wonder of this unbelievable experience have remained with me ever since, nothing can
ever take it away from me" leap from the page. And
again, "I have shared it [an angel experience] with
only a few special friends because it is too precious to
be the subject of scorn, but I have written it now, so
that others may feel more conscious of the presence of
God's angels today."

This is the purpose and challenge of this remarkable book. *Angels* will bring surprise and wonder-
ment, peace and encouragement. It will strengthen
the belief that God Himself is in full control over
what is happening to His creation, the earth and all of
us who inhabit His planet, and that His divine will is
being fulfilled.

# CHAPTER ONE

# *Angels: the Facts*

eathered wings as large as those of eagles, dazzling golden haloes, harps, swords and flowing white robes. These are the traditional images that commonly spring to mind when the subject of angels is raised. The responsibility for this lies largely with great Renaissance artists. As a result, for the vast majority of people, they tend to remain a lifeless concept, because they seem to bear little relation to reality.

As far as the Bible is concerned, its teachings are definite. Angels, according to the Scriptures, are unique spiritual beings who act as messengers and comforters to mankind. In Biblical times they were frequently reported to have been sent by God to give direction or help in time of difficulty to a wide variety of human individuals. They appeared mysteriously, either alone or in groups. They were seen, they spoke and sometimes they sang. Their appearance was awesome, and initially often frightening. After their missions had been fulfilled, equally mysteriously they disappeared.

According to the Bible, angels are an entirely different species from humans. It emphatically tells us not to worship them. No matter how thrilling an angelic visit may be, our praise should be only for God. Among the nearly three hundred Biblical references to angels, some stand out, either because they are more dramatic or because they affect people's lives. For example, God sent an angel to shut the mouths of the hungry lions when Daniel was thrown into their den (Daniel 6:22). Elijah and Jesus were both fed by angels in the wilderness, when there was no food around (1 Kings 19:5—8; Mark 1:13). St. Paul, before he was shipwrecked, was sent an angel to convince him that he would survive (Acts 27:21—6).

These teachings in the context of the Bible are not usually seriously questioned. But in our modern world, an aura of myth and make-believe surrounds the subject of angels. What seems normal and perfectly acceptable in a Biblical context seems irrational and impossible in our everyday lives. In effect, according to popular belief, all possibility of Divine intervention in our worldly affairs, through angels, is rejected. The view of the general public, I am sure, is this: nobody in their right mind would suggest that angels are at work in Great Britain in the 1990s.

To suggest that the opposite is true is to risk being thought unbalanced. It seems crazy, defying all rational analysis in our material world. Nevertheless, there is much evidence to support the view that angels still do exist. Hundreds, possibly thousands, of men and women living today in Great Britain are quite certain they have seen angels. Some even claim to have spoken with them. Invariably, all who have had such an experience feel that their lives have been changed as a result.

It is a curious fact that, despite the references in
the Bible to angels, clergy of all denominations shy
away from mentioning the subject. Even some fully
committed Christians may only discuss their existence tentatively, unsure exactly how angels fit into
their beliefs. Personally I had not doubted their existence, but neither had they featured much in my
thinking. Just before Christmas 1990, however, one
of our church home groups was discussing the appearances of angels to Mary, Joseph and the shepherds, to tell them about the birth of Jesus. Someone
in the group said: "Well, they needed angels then, but
nobody sees angels today, do they?" The group
leader replied that she herself had never seen an angel, but she thought they were still around, and would
find out. The next day she asked me to recommend a
book she could buy on the subject. I told her about
Billy Graham's book, *Angels: God's Secret Agents,*
which is mainly about the Biblical appearances of angels, with just a few up-to-date experiences. I also
had a copy of an American book, *When Angels Appear* by Hope MacDonald, already out of print,
which I lent her, as it included about fifty recent encounters with angels, but that was all I knew of that
was available.

I would have thought no more about it, but over
the next couple of months, everywhere we went the
subject of angels kept coming into conversations, not
raised by us but by other people. This was so notice-
able that my husband and I started saying, "*Someone*
should write a book about people seeing angels today," never for a moment thinking that it should be
one of us.

At the end of February, I went to a Christian con-

ference where one of the speakers was a book publisher, talking about his work and interests. In the
course of his talk, he said that he was always looking
out for people to write about subjects where there
was "a gap in the market." As he said that sentence,
I knew God was speaking into my heart, telling me:
"I have been showing you the need for a book on the
subject of angels for more than two months; now I
am telling you that you are the one to write it; with
My help, get started!" I was amazed. As a non-
author, why should He select me? After an encouraging chat with the publisher following his talk, I began
the research, on March 1, the day after I arrived
home, with great enthusiasm and encouragement
from my family.

The gathering of evidence began by inserting re-
quests in various Christian publications. Asking the
simple question "Have you seen an angel?" produced
a surprisingly large response of personal experiences.
This was picked up by a local newspaper and, as a
result, three local radio stations invited me to be in-
terviewed. This widened the field, as many people
hearing the radio broadcasts had no Church connec-
tion, so would not have read of my request for evidence in any of the Christian publications.

From that time onward, a steady stream of reports
began arriving at my home. They have been sent by
hundreds of obviously sane, down-to-earth people
who described their experiences with a mixture of
awe and reticence. In almost all cases, the conviction
that they have encountered angels is absolute. Two
common factors which noticeably recurred in most
accounts helped underpin their authenticity. Firstly,
all the respondents said the experience had affected

them positively in a deep and lasting way. Furthermore, for most people it was a once-in-a-lifetime experience. Many letters begin with the words, "I have never had another experience like this before or since." This helped convince me that I was not hearing from hypersensitive, over-spiritual people who were always looking out for the extraordinary.

Most incidents have occurred unexpectedly and have been witnessed by people who give every appearance of being honest, ordinary and "not given to fantasy." They happen to people from all levels of society, from all professions and every area of Great Britain, and come from people of every persuasion. For this book, however, I have concentrated on the ones which are in line with the Bible's teaching because I wanted to demonstrate that the angels who feature in the Bible are the same ones that appear to us today.

Many testimonies are about larger-than-life, powerful angels, very different from the rather insipid creatures seen in some artists' impressions down the centuries. This is because an experience of wonder, brilliance and amazement is often difficult to convey. A typical description says, "I saw a huge angel standing astride our driveway. He shone like light. In his hand he held a mighty, drawn sword which also shone." The words "mighty," "huge," "powerful" and "fearless" crop up frequently in the descriptions I have received and they seem to correspond with the fact that angels who appeared in the Bible frequently started their message with "Fear not" or "Don't be afraid." The people in Biblical times who witnessed such awesome sights were, not unnaturally, initially often frightened.

Indeed, some people today who report encounters

with angels say, "I felt frightened at first." But the words spoken, or the sense of peace which accompanied the appearance left them with a great and enduring feeling of comfort. Julian Green, who now lives in Wiltshire, recalls an incident from the 1930s. Julian, then aged six, had just gone to bed and was wondering why the carol "While shepherds watched," which they had been learning at school, said that the shepherds were filled "with mighty dread." "Suddenly there was an angel in the room, a brilliant light, a presence and there might have been wings. I was very much afraid and I understood perfectly about the shepherds. It was a little revelation and I am grateful for it."

When "an angel of the Lord" unexpectedly appeared to that group of shepherds one night on a hillside near Bethlehem, understandably "they were terrified" (Luke 2:9). But they believed the angel's message and rushed to see the newly born Jesus for themselves. Before they did so, the angel giving this important message was joined by "a great company of the heavenly host praising God." This story is widely known, but companies of the heavenly host have been seen on other occasions too. How many people know that "a whole company of angels on a hillside, all praising God" was seen one evening in 1952 at Lee Abbey in North Devon? The vicar's wife, who saw this company of angels, reports, "It was absolutely lovely. But interestingly, like the shepherds, I was a bit afraid to begin with." She and her family had been going through a difficult time so they were tremendously uplifted by hearing she had witnessed this sight of angels praising God.

All the experiences described in this book are from people who were awake at the time. I have sifted out any that could have been dreams. A couple of people have asked to remain anonymous, but the vast majority have not. Some of the reports that follow sound fantastic, but as someone with a double degree and Ph.D. stated: "I have recorded this event with the same faithfulness and respect for truth and accuracy as I would tell it on the witness stand. But even as I record it, I know how incredible it sounds."

A common factor in these accounts is that people say: "I never told anyone, because it seemed too amazing and unbelievable. So I put it to the back of my mind." A few had shared the experience with one or two close friends, others feared they might be thought "over the top." But for some the encounter has been so life-changing that they have felt compelled to share it. Often those they have shared it with have been profoundly affected too.

Catherine Mossey, a housewife from Macclesfield, wrote to tell me of her mother's experience of meeting an angel while in the Manchester Royal Infirmary in December 1991. Her mother, 76-year-old Norah Threader, was due to have a major operation and was greatly worried about it, as she was terrified of dying. "An eight-foot-tall angel appeared in the hospital room, with beautiful ash blond hair. In his right hand he held a huge sword, which he wielded from left to right, as if it weighed no more than a feather. It was an enormous sword with a round guard on the handle. I think he was St. Michael. His wings were beautiful, like the softest down, cream-colored, edged with apricot. He opened his wings slightly and closed them around me, sheltering me from all the evils of the world and I knew then I was safe. He had the most beautiful face I have ever seen, but he was not at all feminine. He was totally masculine and there was such strength about him."

The effect of this experience on Norah was dramatic. Catherine says of her mother: "She was transformed—her fear disappeared. She was filled with the peace that can only come from God, and instead of being anxious, she was joyful." Norah had always lived life to the full, but now that she was dying she told her daughter that she was happier than she had ever been in her life. She lived another four months after the operation, but she never knew fear again, although she had been terrified of dying prior to meeting the angel.

"During those four months, she told her story hundreds of times and it never altered," Catherine remembers, "although Mum's stories were notorious for 'growing' in the telling! This story never grew, because it was true. Everyone who heard of the experience was moved and enriched. Mum always ended her account by saying, 'If you are ever worried or frightened, ask God to help you and He will.' I was privileged to be with her when she died—she smiled!"

As I've said, most of the hundreds of people who responded to my request for reports about angels said they had seen them only once in their lifetime. In some cases they relate incidents that occurred more than seventy years ago. The singularity of the experience suggests that those who responded are rational, sensible and not seeking after strange phenomena. In addition, whether the incident occurred last week or before World War I, it is remembered as clearly as if it happened yesterday. Mr. Ron Hammond, for example, who now lives in Teignmouth, Devon, used to go with his brother to the moors to collect firewood.

One day, during World War I, on their return journey, they were "singing lustily, as boys will," he says. "As we turned the corner, the cemetery could be seen in the distance, with the small chapel in the center of the grounds. Our loud singing petered out, and neither of us spoke until I quietly said to my brother, 'Do you see what I see? It looks like an angel.' We looked together and there, rising quietly above the chapel roof, we could see a white-robed figure. There were no clouds or smoke around, and my brother agreed that we had truly seen an angel."

Mr. Hammond has mulled over the experience many times and concludes, "Was it a sign? The terrible war was soon over, and our father returned from the fighting quite safely. To this day, neither my brother nor myself has forgotten this experience which left a deep impression on our lives."

Donovan Cox had an angel experience during World War II. In the autumn of 1941 London was blitzed for sixty consecutive nights, causing much damage. Donovan and his wife, Doris, lived in Ealing, London, and had sent their son away to boarding school for safety. They had made a downstairs room as safe as possible and slept there at night. One evening, at about 9 P.M., Donovan said to his wife: "There's going to be a disturbance here tonight, but we will be kept safe, so there is no need to worry." Doris asked: "How do you know?" Donovan explained: "I can see an angel above our house protecting us." He saw a huge figure floating about twenty feet above the house in a horizontal position. It had a human shape but was much bigger, wearing a pale-colored cloak, with arms outstretched so it covered the house. He felt as if the whole house was fully protected. Donovan says, "I knew for certain

that the angel was there, and I knew something
would happen that night."

They went to sleep and at about 2 A.M. were awakened by a loud explosion above the house. The doors
were burst open by the blast and there was a sensation of tremendous pressure, as if the window would
come in. The couple closed all the doors and, to their
amazement, found that nothing had been damaged.
Donovan said: "That was it. Everything will be all
right now." They went back to sleep and about 8 A.M.
were visited by the street warden, who had been on
duty all night, on the look-out for bomb damage. He
said: "You had a very lucky escape last night. There
was a parachute bomb descending right over your
house and it exploded in mid-air." This kind of bomb
was designed to explode on impact with the ground,
destroying everything for a large area around. It was
not meant to detonate unless it hit something, so it
should not have exploded harmlessly above the
house. About half an hour later, a firewatcher arrived
with exactly the same report, although the two witnesses had not seen each other, as their stations were
at right angles to each other, the warden's post to
the west of the house, and the firewatching post
to the south, so there could be no doubt about the
precise location of the descending bomb.

Donovan was totally convinced about the angel he
had seen. However, hearing the accounts of two independent witnesses who knew nothing of his vision,
he appreciated just how great God's protection had
been. I was impressed on meeting Mr. Cox at just
how sane and sensible he was; not a man given to visions or fancy, and this is the only such extraordinary
experience that he has ever had.

The fact that not everyone has seen an angel raises

an important question. Why haven't others? There is
no certain answer. It does not mean that those who
have not seen angels are any less spiritual or need
more faith. Some people who have had an angelic
visit have not even been Christian at the time, so
level of faith does not apply, although some of these
people report becoming a believer as a result of the
incident. It seems likely that if God wants you to see
an angel, you will, whether you already believe in
Him or not.

Dot Friend, who attends Bearwood Church near
Bournemouth, has had two experiences of angels;
both sightings occurred when she was attending her
local church. The first happened in about 1987, when
the rector, Ian Savile, asked everyone present to pray
for growth and progress in the Church. They went in
twos and threes to different parts of the church, inside and out, to pray for the congregation and those
living on the housing estate nearby. Dot and another
Christian, Jenny, went outside by the kitchen door to
pray, and as they were praying, Dot saw that two others had joined them. She thought this must be two
other church members, but as the prayer time ended,
the other two were nowhere to be seen, and she was
certain they were angels. At the same time, some-
body else praying with a friend by the front door of
the church also saw an angel while they were praying.

More recently, in early 1992, Dot was praying with
a friend who was distressed about a divisive situation. They were sitting in a car in the church parking
lot. Dot suddenly saw the walls and roof of the
church covered with hordes of angels, of all sizes and
descriptions. She thought it must be a reflection on
the glass, so she wound down the car window, but

this merely meant she saw them even more clearly. Not only did she see them, but she also felt a movement of air, from the gentle fanning of wings, as if among a great flock of birds. Her friend did not see them, but felt reassured when Dot shared what she saw, that the divisive situation would soon be resolved. Dot felt a tremendous surge of hope, a certainty that God was in charge and all would be well, which has remained with her ever since.

These first few highlights of many hundreds of eye-witness accounts serve, I believe, to show that there was good reason for them to be collected together in a book. A clear, orderly collection of some of the vast number of experiences of God at work is necessary to counter-balance the array of literature on the occult which is widely available today.

Most theologians accept that angels exist to carry out God's work, but this is mainly a theoretical understanding. Since researching and writing this book, my conviction has grown that there needs to be a wider knowledge of the existence and activities of God's angels. Among the cascades of letters which have flowed through my mailbox since I appealed for testimonies, many have expressed delight that such a collection is being made, and eagerness to read the experiences of others. The most striking factor in the responses is that an ordinary goodness and honesty shines out of all of them.

Through the evidence of countless personal experiences, this book will show that, however outlandish it sounds at first, angels can and do play a part in today's world. I hope these accounts will evoke in you the same sense of privilege and awe I have felt in receiving them.

# CHAPTER TWO

# *Angels on the Roads*

ne of the surprising features of many reported angel sightings is how relevant and up-to-date they are. An astonishing number of accounts involve vehicles and expressways, which were obviously not part of everyday life in Biblical times!

In March 1991 someone who saw angels on an expressway was fortunately the passenger, not the driver, at the time. June Hutchinson, who lived in Ferndown, Dorset, was traveling with her brother-in-law westward along the M4 to Wales. The previous occasion when he had driven on that road, he had been involved in an accident which had written off his car. Understandably, June was feeling rather nervous, so she silently prayed for safety on the journey. Just then, ahead of them in the sky, June saw two large angels facing each other. They were kneeling, as if in prayer, and wore long flowing white robes. They were beautiful and had huge wings. Although they did not seem to be moving, it appeared, since she watched them for several minutes, that they were traveling along at the same speed as the car. June has never seen angels before or since, so it was totally unexpected. She felt tremendously encouraged, and was sure they would complete their journey safely, which indeed they did.

Another incident that occurred on the road happened to Tina Sturtevant, a young mother and part-time nurse, who, in March 1991, was driving home to Wimborne, Dorset on the Bere Regis road. She was returning from visiting her mother in a nursing home, and was alone in the car. As Tina was driving along, she suddenly heard a voice say, "Stop!" She was so amazed that she braked, and almost immediately a car came around the next corner on her side of the road. It was only because she had stopped, due to the warning, that the other car did not hit her. Its driver managed to regain control and get back to his own side of the road before he reached Tina's car.

Tina knew this road well, and had never previously felt any kind of intuition about danger when driving along it. She is therefore certain that the commanding voice she heard was the voice of an angel warning her and that God had saved her from a certain crash. If, on the other hand, she had *seen* an angel at that moment, Tina thinks the shock might easily have made her crash anyway!

A similar thing happened about thirty years ago to Joan Thomassen, who was driving alone from Lowestoft to Ipswich. Suddenly she heard quite a loud voice shout, "Put your foot on the brake!" She obeyed instantly and, by so doing, avoided a collision with a truck which came around the next bend in the middle of the road. Joan told me: "I am a very down-to-earth person, and not given to imagining things. I have not heard any voices before or since, but it was an unforgettable experience, for which I am very thankful."

I have also received two other accounts of remarkably similar incidents of angel experiences on the road, occurring years apart and in different countries. On each occasion someone was driving alone, late at night, and being tired, started to fall asleep. Both motorists were suddenly roused by a loud voice in the car speaking clearly. In one case the voice said, "Wake up!" and in the other instance, "Watch out!" The effect of both was to prevent an accident. Each driver felt amazed and privileged at what had happened.

Sometimes people feel a sense of intuition or words of guidance. These inner promptings seem to come from God's Holy Spirit. However, when the voice is external, such as clearly heard from the empty back seat of the car, then it appears to be the work of an angel, heard but not seen.

On another occasion the angel was also visible. Tony Olsson is a printer living in Barnstaple. One evening, after an argument, his wife, Jan, drove off in the car dangerously fast. She later said she had felt that she wouldn't have cared if she had killed herself. For some reason, she looked behind her and there, on the back seat, was someone dressed in white. It shook her so much that she pulled over to the side of the road. After waiting until she had calmed down, she went home, but drove carefully this time.

A slightly more dramatic incident happened several years ago to three people together. Peggy Sims, who lived near Exeter, was learning to drive and was on an outing to Woodbury Common. Peggy was being instructed by her husband and a friend was sitting in the back seat. Unfortunately, she turned a corner too fast, the car mounted a bank and tipped over on to the road. To all three of them, however, it felt as though the car was being supported by unseen hands, so that it was very gradually and gently let down until it was on its side on the road. Nothing was damaged: there wasn't even a cracked window. No one was shocked or injured in the slightest. All felt certain they had been protected by an unseen angel.

An elderly gentleman in Cornwall wrote to tell me about an incident which happened as long ago as 1920. Harry Thompson, who now lives in St. Austell, writes: "I was riding a motorbike to Ilfracombe, with my wife, Edith, traveling in the side-car. Beyond South Molton, we drove into a thick, white mist, so the visibility was limited. I was going downhill, when suddenly the steering was taken out of my control. The machine was steered safely, by unseen hands, around a hairpin bend that I had not been able to see in the thick mist." Harry has never forgotten how God saved the lives of himself and his wife so unexpectedly that day.

One morning in August 1990, when Alan and Susan Walker and their family were setting off on vacation, they had an unusually protracted start to their journey. Leaving their home in Thetford, Norfolk, they had only traveled a mile when they heard an awful sound and, looking back, saw the caravan they were towing tilting at an alarming angle. To their horror they found the wheel studs had sheared off, leaving the wheel jammed under the caravan. Unhitching the car, they drove home to see if they could track down a replacement wheel.

While Alan phoned garages, Susan drove back to the caravan to get the dimensions of the wheel. All the way she was praying frantically, "O Lord, please

help, oh please." As she rounded the corner and the
caravan came into view, she saw an angel on the roof
of the van, nonchalantly seated with his crossed legs
dangling over the side. The smiling figure held a
sword in his hand. Never having seen an angel before, Susan burst into tears, but at the same time she
heard the words, "There is no problem here, we have
the victory."

There then followed a succession of what Susan
describes as "God's little coincidences," starting with
a friend unexpectedly driving past who stopped to see
if he could help. The first thing needed was a low
loader to get the caravan away from the grassy bank
it was jammed against, in order to replace the wheel.
The nearest one they knew of was twenty-five miles
away. The friend who stopped had seen another
friend that morning using a low loader he had hired!
He set off in pursuit of him, and found him almost
immediately, driving along the road. He discovered,
even more remarkably, that the low loader was
owned by the little garage just at the top of the road
from where the caravan was stuck. Aubrey, the me-
chanic, brought the low loader, which also had a
winch, and they managed to get the caravan back
home.

Finding replacement studs presented more of a
problem as the caravan was old, but the first person
they telephoned knew where to get them. Susan reports: "There was a real cry of joy as they were replaced on the van, and we were able to finally set off
at six in the evening for our holiday." They traveled
down to Somerset for a Christian camp called New
Wine, praising God for all His care shown to them
that day.

A few years ago, Sandra Pike and her family were

driving from their home in Stafford to visit her parents in Wolverhampton. Halfway on the journey, her husband stopped the car and changed seats so Sandra could have some driving practice. She was rather nervous as she hadn't driven for a while, so she prayed for God's protection and help to enable her to drive well. Suddenly Sandra was aware that a very tall angel was standing by the driver's door. His robe went down to his feet and he carried a sword at his side. As they drove along, the angel continued to stand beside the car, without seeming to be moving, although they were traveling at 40 mph. Sandra says: "I didn't understand this, but I knew it to be true: we moved while he stood still, but he continued to watch over us."

A totally different kind of protection was afforded to Christine Bearman as she was driving her daughter to a tennis coaching lesson on the morning of Thursday, August 2, 1988. Christine, who was in a Mini, was involved in an accident with a Volvo. Anticipating the impact, with all her heart and strength Christine screamed, "Please God help us!" Suddenly, she felt "someone" in the car with them and in the middle of the windscreen there appeared a circle of very bright yellow light. Christine had the feeling of utter peace and of being kept safe. The windscreen stayed intact and, although shocked, she and her daughter were not injured. The car was badly crushed but Christine reports: "It was a miracle we weren't killed or badly injured, and I truly believe that God sent an angel that day to protect us, and the sign was the circle of bright yellow light on the windscreen."

Another experience connecting the color yellow with angels occurred in Cumbria about ten years ago during a snowstorm. Elsie Hedger was returning home to Keswick with her father, whom she had taken to Carlisle for an eye check-up. The other passengers in the car were an elderly friend, who often recalls the following experience, and a solicitor and his wife from London, who were being taken to Keswick.

In the difficult driving conditions, Elsie took a wrong turn and found they were on the moorland road. Since she knew it would be treacherous in the blizzard conditions, she felt it was unwise to go on. Two other cars were behind, and as she began to reverse so did the other cars until they all reached a crossroads. "Decision time! Did we go all the way back to Carlisle, or risk taking the road to the left which I did not know? I knew that if we did not get off the moors soon, we would be stranded. I said, 'What we need is a snowplow!' I had just got the words out of my mouth when what should appear to the right of us but a big yellow snowplow! The biggest I have ever seen. A friendly voice asked, 'Where do you want to go?' When I told him, he said, 'Follow me.' So, off down the road to the left we followed the snowplow. Just behind the line of cars came a little yellow van, which seemed to be 'protecting' us on our journey, in case we faltered on the slippery snow. When we finally reached the main road, I was pointed in the direction of Keswick, this road having been cleared and now safe to travel on. When I tried to thank the drivers of the two vehicles which had escorted us to safety, they had disappeared, snowplow, van and all! The road was straight for a long way in either direction, but they were nowhere to be seen. I asked all my passengers if any of them had seen which way the vehicles had gone, but none of them had seen them leave. They had simply vanished."

The elderly friend, Elsie and her father had all been praying when in the predicament on the moors. They all firmly believed that the vehicles were an answer to their prayers, and that the drivers must have been angels, since they disappeared without trace, as soon as the job was done. Elsie concludes: "The moors are treacherous at a time like that, and only the Lord could have helped us out of the difficulty."

Janice Davies, of Bournville, Birmingham, had an unusual experience of protection when she was about fourteen years old. She lived in the Wanstead area of London then and was cycling to her piano lesson one Saturday afternoon. Janice describes the event: "At the traffic lights I had to turn right, but I foolishly decided to rush around when the lights were changing to red. I have a very clear memory of the next few seconds. My front wheel went down a pot-hole in the road, my bike tipped to the right, and I knew I was going to be thrown into the path of a truck. Then I was aware of a supporting feeling under my right arm, as if someone's hand was holding me and lifting me up. The bike resumed its upright position, and I continued safely on my way. It was amazing—I just knew there was someone looking after me."

Lawrence Ball remembers clearly what happened when he was riding home from work on his motorbike in the summer of 1950. As he rode toward Hamworthy, Poole, where he lived, a large car overtook him. It suddenly turned sharply in front of him to enter a gateway to the left. There was no way Lawrence could avoid hitting the side of the car as it was so close. Just as he was anticipating the impact, he felt a huge hand gently hold back both himself

and the motorbike. He seemed suspended until the
danger was past and he could continue his journey.
He knew something miraculous had happened, beyond his own control.

Sometimes a warning is given that something serious is going to occur. This happened to Katharine
Wood, a Baptist and mother of three from Somerset,
who was driving her Mini in the New Forest, taking
the children for a visit to their grandmother. Katharine reports that she had the feeling of an impending
accident, but was certain that she and her three children would be kept safe. As if to confirm this, she
then saw "four angels, one at each corner of the car,
traveling along with us." A couple of days later, on
the journey home, a car further ahead turned suddenly. All the following cars braked, but in the heavy
rain, they concertinaed into one another. Incredibly,
Katharine's Mini was only slightly damaged, and nobody in the car was hurt or even shocked. Katharine
believes this is the only time she has ever seen angels. She is grateful to God for the special protection
He gave her family that day.

The following incident also happened in the 1950s.
A Nottingham GP, Dr. John Graham, was driving
home after a busy evening surgery through dense fog
with visibility of only about two yards. He knew the
road well, but progress was slow, and he frequently
had to stop and start. "About halfway home," Dr.
Graham reports, "I found myself, to my horror, driving on the wrong side of the road, facing possible on-
coming traffic." He was soon aware of a "presence"
sitting beside him in the passenger seat. He continues: "My eyes were glued to the road, but my feeling
of panic left me and I was aware of a sense of amazing calm. I was able to rejoin the correct line of traf-

fic and for that brief time there had not been any on-coming vehicles.

"When I eventually got home and related the experience to my wife, she said, 'Oh, Fiona [then aged seven] was praying for you that you would have a safe journey home.' Together, we calculated that the angelic 'presence' came around the same time as Fiona's prayer." It seems that, because of the prayer, God intervened to prevent a probable accident, by restoring peace through sending an angel.

In another traffic incident, serious injury was again prevented when it seemed unavoidable. Joyce Wilmshurst reports that she was cycling over the common to her home in Reigate, Surrey. A motorist coming down a side road did not stop at the junction with the main road and drove straight into Joyce on her bicycle. She says: "There was a bang, as the car hit the bicycle, and I felt myself falling, unable to free my feet, which were trapped. I looked at the radiator of the car and thought, 'Now I am going to die.' I then felt myself being lifted up, and I looked down on the blue hood of the car and the upturned faces of some men."

When Joyce opened her eyes, she found she was not in Heaven as expected, but lying on the warm road. She felt no pain and found she could sit up. She expected her feet to look a horrible sight, but they only had abrasions and bruises. Joyce continued: "The driver carried me to a seat and retrieved my glasses and shoes. When I looked at the soles of my shoes, there were black tire marks on them, made by the car wheels."

Of this miraculous escape, she concludes: "My feet were not in the shoes when the car drove over them, as I was being lifted up by angels and laid safely on the road some distance away." Her belief in angels is now unswerving.

Angela Graham-Collins, who lives near Cirencester, Gloucestershire, was driving home from a Christian home group one dark, wet evening. She had been involved in a car accident a few weeks earlier so was feeling rather anxious. Her ten-year-old son, Rowan, who was in the back seat, suddenly said, "It's OK, Mum, we have got three angels in the car." He said they were about six inches high, with gold hair and light flowing from them, dancing around the rear-view mirror. His mother did not see them, but she felt very peaceful and knew she and her son would return home safely.

These examples show that angels are always ready to help us. God sends them to protect us in situations from which we cannot escape. Accidents happen so quickly on the roads that we may not have time to prevent them, and we need help from outside ourselves. With traffic on the roads ever increasing, we can be thankful that these messengers from God are always available to us.

## CHAPTER THREE

# *The Angel Experiences of Children*

hildren have a natural capacity for believing that what they see before them is true. Adults tend to rationalize and question, especially if they see something which does not fit with their own ideas and understanding. On seeing an angel in their bedroom, for example, an adult may disregard it as being a dream or the figment of an over-active imagination, or the result of a piece of cheese eaten before bedtime. A child's mind, on the other hand, is uncluttered by such rationalization. He accepts as fact what he sees before his eyes. He is glad to see an angel and happily tells an adult about it. When this is dismissed as fantasy, he keeps it to himself, but he never forgets it. He knows it is special and real. He just does not talk about it, so other adults are not able to undermine what he knows to be the truth.

Such was the case of James Draper who is now a canon of the Church of England in Humberside, but was only five when he had an angel experience. James was traveling by car with his family in their old "Essex four-door." He was leaning against the door which opened and he fell out. He writes, "My vivid impression of that moment is with me as I write some sixty-two years later. I was outside the car and falling, and with me was a figure in white. The seconds before I hit the ground and passed out seemed an age, so it was very reassuring to have that white angel with me." James had a fractured skull and was in the hospital for some time, but as the car was traveling at some speed, it was remarkable that he was not killed. He relates the family's reaction: "It was suggested, when I was recounting the experience to my family later, that I was confusing the events, and the figure in white was a nurse at the hospital. But I know what I know! The angel was definitely outside the car waiting for me when I fell."

Many people are comfortable with the thought that guardian angels are protecting children. Jesus spoke of angels guarding children in Matthew 18:10 when He said: "See that you do not look down on one of these little ones. For I tell you that their angels in heaven always see the face of My Father in heaven." They assume, however, that they leave us as we grow up. But that is not the case. Psalm 91:11 tells us: "God will put His angels in charge of you to protect you wherever you go." This is for all believers, not just children.

In 1909 two young sisters who saw an angel in the sky were readily believed by their family, perhaps because there were two of them, or maybe because they were so emphatic about their experience. Gladys Ruffle who then lived in Fernhurst, Sussex, was seven and had gone up to bed with her sister, Gwen, on

Christmas Eve. They both went to sleep, but Gladys
woke during the night and roused her sister to see if
their Christmas stockings had yet been filled. They
had not, so the two little girls prepared to snuggle
down again when their attention was caught by something in the sky. They both sat on the edge of the bed
and, through the window, witnessed an incredible
sight.

Gladys describes what they saw: "In the sky were
two golden doves which were flying very close to
each other and, as their wings touched, the figure of
an angel appeared, surrounded by an aura of radiance. It was quite breathtaking! Dumbfounded, we
just sat in complete awe. The angel vanished and the
golden doves gradually faded into the sky. We were
not frightened, but we could not speak for a while,
being enraptured by the whole scene. Realization
suddenly dawned upon us that this was something
very unusual."

Gladys and Gwen called their mother, who rushed
up the stairs and was perturbed to find them so excited. The incident was the girls' sole topic of conversation for days afterwards, so their parents
recognized how important it was to them. The girls
knew they had been privileged to see something very
precious.

Jan Hawkes was only four when, swimming with
her family in a pool in a river, she nearly drowned.
"I began to sink and got tangled up on the river bed.
I was aware of a golden light and angels around
me. I don't know how I would have known they were
angels at that age. My father saved me from drown-
ing, but I've always remembered the incident clearly
to this day."

Megan Watkins, at the age of nine, ran right into

an angel. She and her brother were running across their lawn when she suddenly saw a silver-white angel, about seven or eight feel tall, standing beneath a monkey puzzle tree. From her home in Raglan, Wales, Megan describes what she saw that day: "I distinctly noticed the wings folded at the back. The angel was holding out a sword in front of me, and I could not stop running. I thought I would be killed, but I felt nothing."

Release from fear is just as necessary for children as physical protection. A little girl of six and a half was at the boarding school run by her four spinster aunts. They were good ladies, but strict on discipline, so when young Norah awoke after a nightmare she had to learn to cry quietly until she could sleep again. One night she had a nightmare about a fierce black horned dog which was attacking her. "I woke in terror to find the apparent likeness of the dog silhouetted in the moonlight on the wall behind my bed. In an agony of fear, I closed my eyes, clasped my hands and gasped out the little prayer I had learned:

> *Lord, keep me safe this night;*
> *Secure from all my fears.*
> *May angels guard me while I sleep,*
> *Till morning light appears."*

Norah continues: "As I opened my eyes I saw, bending over me, a figure with a beautiful head and long, colorful feathered wings. As soon as it vanished, I *knew* I had seen an angel who was there to keep me safe. The dog shadow had gone, and I had such a lovely feeling as I quietly lay there, no longer afraid. In the morning when I told my aunts they were extraordinarily kind to me as they questioned me and listened to me intently. The memory of seeing this beautiful angel has never left me, and I have no doubt that I was really awake, not dreaming. It has been a joy throughout my life that God sent one of His messengers to quieten the fears of a trembling, troubled child." Norah de la Mare Norris now lives in Bradford-on-Avon, Wiltshire, and describes herself as "a very ordinary elderly woman" who has told the experience to many children during her teaching years.

Sometimes angels have appeared to children not to rescue but to encourage them. As a small child, Joan Cooper was kneeling by her bed to pray, when she saw an angel, also kneeling, beside her. She did not look up to see the face, but reached out and felt the hem of the angel's garment in her hand. Joan grew up in Australia, but now lives in Seaton, Devon, and is a friend of mine.

Another of my friends, Alison Lechler, saw an angel in her garden in Lincolnshire when she was six years old. At the end of a happy summer's day, Alison lay in bed watching the changing colors of the sky through the open window. "As I looked out at the large apple tree where that day I had mastered the art of tree climbing, I saw a shining form standing on top of the tree, with its arms raised as if praising God. I do not recall seeing it come or go, but when my mother came up, I described it all to her in the matter-of-fact manner of a child who has no reason to question such an event. She is a Christian and she believed what I had seen."

Another six-year-old who saw an angel from her bed lived in a small cottage in a village in north-east Wales. Money was short and tempers often shorter, so young Maggie would sometimes be sent to bed early, where she felt abandoned in the cold dark bedroom. She would lie, rigid with fear, thinking of the stories of "the bogeyman" which her big brother had told her. One evening in the darkness, Maggie saw a glow at the foot of the bed. She explains, "I watched, fascinated, as it grew. The glow spread until it was huge, stretching up as high as the ceiling and as wide as my bed. Slowly and quietly the figure of an angel appeared in the middle of the glow. I had the most wonderful feeling of safety and well-being. The angel was beautiful, all in sparkling white, with a lovely kind smiling face, golden hair and a pair of huge wings which swept up and curved over his back, sleek with white feathers. I don't know how long he stayed, but the next thing I remember was my mother coming into the room, giving me a smack and thrusting me back into bed. I told her I was looking for angel feathers on the floor, which got me another smack. I was then left alone in the dark, but now it didn't matter because I had seen an angel. I knew Jesus had sent him and I was safe."

David Wills and his sister Margaret also saw angels in their bedroom, in this case during World War II. They lived in Croxley Green, near Watford, Hertfordshire, with their mother and grandparents, who were all Christians. Their father was in the RAF and their home was in sight of the nightly bombings on London in the Blitz from September 1940 to May 1941.

David reports what he recalls of one night when he was five: "I was woken up during the night by an extremely bright light in the bedroom and a feeling of discomfort in my legs. As I cracked open my eyes in the brightness, I saw a figure sitting on my bed, in fact, sitting on my legs! The figure was the source of

the bright light and I immediately knew it was an angel. I was greatly amazed, but not frightened. It was
at least adult human size, with two folded wings. It
wore a sort of robe, but everything about it seemed to
emit light. It was not looking at me and did not seem
aware that I was watching it. I found its presence—
and weight—very reassuring. I can remember the following morning telling my mother, and she showed
great interest in the story. She remembers it clearly,
even today, because the remarkable thing was that
she had spent the whole of that very night in prayer,
asking God to guard and protect her family."

This was obviously a prayer-filled home, so it is
perhaps not surprising that David's sister Margaret
also saw an angel in the early years of the war. Margaret remembers one night when she was about four
years old. Soon after her mother's bedtime prayers
and goodnight kiss, Margaret saw a very bright light
at the foot of the bed. The light became an angel,
which went out of the door and along the passage.
Margaret's bed was near the door, so without leaving
her bed, she was able to crane her neck and see the
angel continuing down the passage. She had no doubt
that they would all be protected during the conflict,
and she saw the angel in her bedroom on more than
one occasion.

Two people have told me they saw angels in vicar-
ages during World War II. One was the Vicar's
daughter, the youngest of three children, who was
rather anxious about leaving home in Alton, Hampshire, to go to boarding school. While Alison lay
awake one night, an angel, dressed all in gold, came
and stood at the end of the bed. The angel said:
"Don't worry, everything will be all right." Twelve-
year-old Alison sat up in bed and touched the place

where the angel had stood. Due to that event, boarding school was a very happy period for her, which has had a strong influence for good on her life.

The other vicarage incident occurred to Mary Atherton who was evacuated to Rainow, a small village in Cheshire. To a small seven-year-old, the rambling old house seemed enormous. Mary was always frightened in the dark, and while in bed she held on tightly to the sheets. One night she awoke feeling something gently stroking her head. She timidly pulled back the sheet and, looking to the right, saw a figure in white kneeling beside the bed. "All the time I watched the figure it did not move, but I felt a bit frightened and started to run out of the room. When I looked back, the figure had gone. I soon realized it was an angel sent to comfort me and I quickly lost my fear of the dark. The memory of this has always remained with me very vividly in the fifty years since. Isn't it so like the Lord to comfort one of His children upset by separation from family?"

Sometimes an angel comes to give a message we should hear. Kim Spicer was walking home from school in the village of Elstead, Surrey, when he was about seven years old. A very tall winged angel appeared to him, dressed in white. He told Kim that his mother was going to have a baby. He was very excited, as he had two sisters, but longed for a brother. Surprisingly, he said nothing about this when he arrived home but, a few days later, his mother told Kim that she was going to have a baby, so the angel's message was confirmed.

In December 1991 ten-year-old Natalie Raitt of Aberdeen was working at her school desk as usual when she looked up and saw three angels kneeling on white steps. She said they were smiling at her, wore long white gowns and had bare feet. As a sequel to that, about a month later on three successive evenings, Natalie heard angels singing. On each occasion she was in the bathroom and the third time she sensed many angels all around her, although she could not see them.

Another child who has described seeing angels quite matter-of-factly is Paul Maguines of Belfast. He lives in a Christian home, but angels have not been emphasized in any way, by his parents, or at school or Sunday school. Yet Paul, only five and a half, has talked of seeing angels in the room when Christian music is being played, and of an angel standing beside a Christian friend of his mother. Paul's mother asked him if he was frightened when he saw them. He replied, "Never, Mum, their faces are beautiful. I never feel afraid, just happy."

In August 1992 Harry Humphries, aged thirteen, was camping with his family in New Wine, the Christian camp in Somerset. He was walking back alone to the tent when suddenly in front of him was a great dazzling light. Harry says, "An angel stood about eight meters in front of me; it made me jump and my heart missed a beat. It stood about seven feet high with its arms outstretched and a smile on its face. It seemed to be male, but I couldn't really tell. It was all dressed in white with long golden hair and wings folded behind. I felt it was a sign that God was there with me."

Alan Wilkinson, who is now in his twenties, lives in Ringwood, Hampshire. As a young child he was often ill, and it was thought he would not survive. Once when he was four and very poorly, Alan called out to his parents during the night. When they came into his room, he said he had just seen a white angel, holding a large book and gold pen. The angel showed Alan his name written in the book; he told Alan he would get better because it was not time for him to go to heaven yet.

At Christmas 1926 six-year-old Peggy Harding was in a coma due to a very high fever. She explains: "The doctor said I could not possibly recover. My mother and her friend, who were both praying for me, said that I would! A week later I awoke and sat up in bed. While I was semi-conscious my mother and her friend had both heard me speak about angels. When visitors came to our home after that I would always want to take them to a nearby cemetery to point out the statues of angels!" Peggy now lives near Wells, Somerset, and remembers clearly this childhood event.

Marie Sutton was sixteen when she became very ill during a serious flu epidemic, which claimed many lives. She remembers her mother coming into the bedroom on Friday, November 11, 1918, to tell her that World War I was over, and she heard the church bells ringing in celebration. The next day her condition worsened and she recalls her family's concern with quiet talking and sobs in the passageway when the doctor came to see her.

Mrs. Sutton says, "Quite suddenly, at the far end of the room, a company of angels appeared singing, 'Glory to God, Alleluia,' gradually coming nearer to me. I had the feeling they had come for me and I was suddenly very happy. They stayed for a few minutes and then vanished, leaving me feeling sad that they had gone. At the same time, the doctor said to my mother, 'The crisis has passed; she is going to be all right.' I was sad that the angels had gone, but when

I opened my eyes, my father hugged me saying, 'Thank the Lord.' "

Both Alan Wilkinson and Peggy Harding and their parents were assured of their recovery by the angelic visits. In Marie's case, she thought they signified her going to heaven, but she discovered that the angels' message meant that she was needed to continue to serve God in this life. Her two children have both served the Lord as ministers of the Church and Mrs. Sutton has always been thankful for the angels' visit. Sometimes, however, just as much comfort is received by the patient and their family when angels surround a dying child. In 1930, a much-loved, pretty little girl was dying of tuberculosis. Her schoolfriend, David Hadlow, who grew up in the same village, Lenham near Maidstone, Kent, but who now lives in Portsmouth, wrote to tell me about her. Her name was Pretoria Green and the ten-year-old was such a kind and gentle child that her death was a great shock to the whole school.

It was customary then to keep the open coffin in a downstairs room from the death until the funeral, so friends and neighbors could come to the house to pay their last respects. David went with some other schoolfriends and they were all amazed that her face looked so radiant and smiling. Pretoria's mother then told the children of her last words just before she passed away. "Oh, Mummy, everything is ever so beautiful and bright. I can see so many lovely flowers and the angels are singing. Mummy, it's wonderful."

Another girl who died of the same illness also saw an angel in the room at the moment of her death. Minnie Gibson was nineteen when the end came—in Belfast in about 1929. Her mother was sitting at her bedside when Minnie pointed to the corner of the room saying, "Look, Mother." Her mother saw nothing unusual, so she asked her daughter what she could see. Minnie replied, "An angel, a beautiful angel." Shortly afterward, she died peacefully.

Ten-year-old Ann Janney of Grimsby was lying in bed at bedtime when an angel appeared in her room. She called her mother, but when she came in Ann said: "Oh, Mum, you missed it; an angel was here." Elsie, her mother, asked what it was like. Ann replied, "Well, it came with a lot of light all around it, and sat on my window-sill, but when you were coming up it disappeared." When she became a mother herself, Ann told her three children about the angel who visited her.

Someone else whose angel experience made a lasting impression on them was Moira Salman, who now lives in Lincolnshire. In 1942, Moira, then aged eleven, was in the local hospital having her tonsils removed. As it was wartime, sweets, fruit and chocolate were in very short supply. In the bed opposite was a lovely lady who each day sent across to Moira a treat such as an apple or a few squares of chocolate.

One night, Moira woke in the middle of the night to see a very bright light. She says, "It seemed to fill the whole ward, so I half sat up and, to my astonishment, I saw two angels! They were high above the kind lady's bed, with their arms outstretched toward her, looking down. I saw them as two complete figures, with shining faces and long hair, and light surrounding their heads like haloes. They wore white robes and, although I did not see wings, I can understand why they are often portrayed with wings, as they were suspended high above the bed, almost at the ceiling. The following morning the bed was empty and I knew the kind lady had died.

"When my mother next visited me she asked where the lady had been moved to. Immediately I replied, 'She died in the night, Mummy.' A bit annoyed in case I should be upset, my mother later spoke to the ward sister asking why I had been told someone had died. The sister replied, 'No one told your daughter about it.' Concerned, my mother asked me 'How did you know the lady had died?' She was amazed by my reply: 'I saw the angels come to get her.' "

Moira concludes her account: "I became a nursing sister myself, and have seen many people die, but I have never witnessed another angel. I like to think they were comforting me about death, as well as the lady they came for."

Angels appearing to comfort as well as protect were seen by Chris Gillott, who lives in Hemel Hempstead. In 1986 Chris went with a party of other schoolfriends and a teacher as the "advance guard" to set up the school summer camp in Ilfracombe, Devon. It was a very blustery evening, but by nightfall they had succeeded in putting up a tent.

During a thunderstorm in the night, Chris and his friend, Matthew, woke up. Instead of lightning, they saw a bright light continuously shining all around their tent. Since they were in the middle of a field during a stormy night they thought the light rather strange so they opened the tent flap. Angels, very tall beings dressed in white, stood all around the tent. The light was shining from them, and immediately one of the boys thought of verse 7 in Joshua 1. The other looked it up: "Be strong and very courageous." They knew the angels were a sign that God was with them and, feeling at peace, they both went straight to sleep.

All these people, whether still children or now

grown up, are certain of the truth of what they saw.
Again, the majority have had only one angel experience, which is the same pattern as for adults, and
seems to confirm that they are not fanciful or unusual
people.

# CHAPTER FOUR

# *Angels in Human Form*

From the evidence of many accounts, it seems that when God chooses to send an angel, it need not always appear in traditional form. Often it may be more appropriate for the angel to appear in the guise of a human, since flowing robes and wings may sometimes be a hindrance when helping to rescue or guide someone! What distinguishes these angels from people is that after they have completed the job they came to do, they immediately disappear. They are suddenly "gone" or may even vanish before the person's eyes. The following incidents speak for themselves.

Richard and Basil were preparing for a Scripture Union summer camp where they were to be assistant leaders. Their task for this particular day was to transport canoes to the river Avon and unload them from a trailer, parked on the Dundas aqueduct over a disused canal. "The canal," says Richard, "was closed, as it was rather a remote location." Unfortunately Basil reversed the towing vehicle awkwardly and a back wheel went over the edge of the canal. It was impossible for the two of them on their own to get the heavy vehicle back on to the road because of the steep drop down to the canal. Richard says, "I was certainly praying quietly in my heart, and I am sure Basil was."

Both had just decided that they must walk back to the school where they were staying, about a mile away, to get help when suddenly two men, in checked shirts, appeared from nowhere and jumped over a fence to help them. Without a word, the newcomers lifted the vehicle and pushed it clear. But before Richard and Basil could thank them, they disappeared as quickly as they had come. They were rugged, strong-looking angels, most appropriate for the task! As Richard concluded, "They seemed to approximate far more to Biblical angels than to the angels we see in art." They were certain these unexpected helpers were angels because of the way they appeared just when needed and disappeared immediately, without any verbal communication.

Bob Heasman also encountered a human angel when he went to visit an employee who had been off sick for a while. He had the address, in Aylesbury, but could not find the way as the town was unfamiliar to him. He prayed, "Lord, where do I go?" and heard a voice say, "Turn left." He did, and drove along a long straight road. Again he asked, "Lord help me," and then noticed a woman standing on the pavement. He drove past—but then felt constrained to turn the car around and pulled up alongside her. Surprisingly, she said, "I knew you would come back." Bob gave her the address he was trying to find and she gave him the following precise instructions: "Take the second left, and when you come to a

T-junction, the house is right opposite." Bob thanked
her and got into the car. She waved and disappeared
before his eyes.

Jeannie Morgan was looking for a large quantity of
foam to re-cover all the seats in an old coach, which
she and her husband, Ken, intended to use as a coffee
bar for teenagers. Through a friend, she was given
the phone number of someone who would give them
the foam free of charge. She therefore arranged to
meet this man, who was a stranger to her, at a particular spot in town, so they could go to the warehouse
for the foam. He said it would be easy for her to spot
him as "It is never busy in that part of town on a Saturday."

However, when Jeannie reached the agreed meeting place, she was dismayed to discover a festival
taking place with morris dancers and people milling
about everywhere. She waited for about half an hour
but couldn't see anyone who appeared to be looking
for a stranger. Jeannie remembers, "I felt very foolish
and kept praying for help. Then an ordinary-looking
man stopped in front of me and said, 'Are you looking for Alan Beatley?' In amazement I replied,
'Yes—how did you know?' He then said, 'He is in
the pub over there; I will go and get him for you.'
When Alan came over to me I said, 'I'm glad that
your friend came over to get you; I was just about to
go home.' Alan said, 'That wasn't my friend—I've
never seen him before. I thought he was someone
you knew as he used your name.' I had certainly not
told him my name, nor the name of the person I was
looking for, which he also knew. We both declared
that it must have been a angel which Jesus sent to
help us find one another."

Perhaps an even more astonishing incident was the

arrival of an angel plumber! Patricia Heaton, a single parent, was living in Yorkshire with her two small children when her gas boiler broke down. Not only was there no hot water, Patricia was also concerned about the danger of an explosion. That morning, she telephoned numerous plumbers to ask for estimates, but they were all far more than she could afford. She gave none of them her address or phone number. Worried about the danger aspect, with young children in the house, she prayed for help. Within half an hour, there was a plumber on the doorstep. How did he know? She had told nobody. Patricia was too stunned to ask him. She showed him the boiler and while he was mending it, she worried about how she was going to pay him. On his way out, she asked, "How much do I owe you?" "That's all right, love, have it on me," was his surprising reply. Patricia quickly followed him, to thank him, but he had vanished. No car, not a soul in sight, he had disappeared! Patricia thanked God for the way He had so unexpectedly sent the help she needed.

Someone else who had an unexpected visitor was Isabel Walton, who is a Methodist lay preacher in Kineton near Coventry. In 1990 she was studying for her lay preacher qualification as well as doing a full-time job and caring for her husband and two children. One day when she was at home trying to write an essay with a migraine coming on, she felt tired and fed up. She put on some background music to help her concentration. Just then a uniformed official of the Midlands Electricity Board arrived to read the meter. Isabel invited him in and offered him some coffee. While sitting in the kitchen drinking the coffee, he noticed that the music playing was from Taizé, a Christian community in France, who have a unique style of singing. In a soft Irish accent, he said he had spent time in the Veritas Community in Ireland, similar to Taizé, which he described as "next to heaven."

They talked for some time, having a great deal in common and each talking about their relationship with the Lord. He stressed to her the importance of prayer for all who wished to move on with God. The conversation with this gentle middle-aged man with twinkling eyes left Isabel feeling better and much refreshed. She explains, "He smiled, shook my hand and left. Then I remembered that he had not read the meter, so I went next door, but he wasn't there. The other neighbors had not seen him either and none of them had had their meters read that day. There was no van or electricity man anywhere about. This man had led me back to God, which I needed. We had talked about Jesus, and his coffee cup was empty. Yet no one else had seen him. Was he an angel? I most surely say he was, and I shall never forget his smiling face and twinkling eyes."

In Genesis 18, Abraham was sitting at the entrance to his tent one day when he "looked up and saw three men standing nearby." He invited the travelers to come in for a meal and talked with them while his wife was preparing it. He had prayed to God for a son, since his wife was childless, and these visitors surprised him by telling him that Sarah would have a son the following year. One of the three, who later in the chapter is described as being the Lord, then told Abraham God's plans for the punishment of wicked people in nearby towns. The other two travelers, Abraham realized after they had left, were angels. In the light of this experience, Hebrews 13:2 warns us: "Do not forget to entertain strangers, for by so doing some people have entertained angels without knowing it."

Early in 1978, Bruce Humphrey, who now lives near Wimborne, in Dorset, had an argument with his grown-up son, David. It was complicated in that Bruce and his wife were living in America, while David and his family were in England. Several months of angry, transatlantic correspondence hurt both of them deeply, and the situation worsened. As a Christian, Bruce knew it was wrong for him to be at odds with his son for so long and in November he decided to apologize and make peace. He sat down and wrote a letter to David, offering forgiveness and asking him in his turn to forgive his father. Something remarkable happened: while his letter was still in the mail to England, he received an almost identical letter from David.

Bruce immediately wanted to see David and make peace face to face so he telephoned him at once saying, "Can I come over to visit you for the weekend?" David was delighted, so Bruce made plans to travel the next day. He phoned the John F. Kennedy airport to book a ticket, but was told just to come to the airport next day and get a stand-by flight. Bruce was shocked, therefore, when he arrived at the airport to find the TWA booking office thronging with three or four hundred people, all trying to get flights to England. Heathrow airport, it transpired, had been fogbound the previous day and the backlog of delayed flights now meant that no seats were available on any flight to London. Bruce spent the next three frustrating hours in lines at every other airline office before eventually returning to the TWA booking hall where the situation seemed just as hopeless as before.

Just then, an official wearing a blazer came in and

walked straight up to Bruce, asking, "Can I help you?" "I'm trying to get to London," Bruce replied, "but it's hopeless. Every flight is fully booked." The man looked at the clipboard he was carrying and said, "I have two seats available at 8:30 P.M." Bruce could not believe his ears. He paid the man and received both a ticket and some advice: "Ignore the crowds," the official said. "You'll find a porter outside." As soon as Bruce left the booking hall, a tall man came over to him. It was an unusual place to find a porter, but he took Bruce's luggage, gave him a boarding pass and was gone, luggage and all. Bruce was dumbfounded! It seemed like a con. But the ticket was valid, the seat on the plane was booked in his name and his luggage was in London when he arrived.

Bruce is in no doubt that the two men who helped him were angels. As far as he is concerned there is no other explanation. Why else should two over-stretched airline officials, who had far too much business at their desks, suddenly single out one passenger? Bruce had a very special reunion with his son, and thanked God for the heavenly intervention which made it possible.

In another account reported to me, the assistance came from an equally unexpected source. Esther Vera Lever, who does voluntary work in Israel, was traveling to stay with a friend overnight in East Grinstead. As she was returning the next day to Israel, she had a large amount of luggage with her. The journey necessitated her changing trains at Easy Croydon, but she had far too much to carry on her own.

"I discovered," she reports, "that I had only a minute to get from one platform to the other, and I despaired of getting all my baggage there. At that moment, a young man came running up, picked up most of it, and told me to bring the rest and follow him. Off we went, through an underpass, up a ramp and on to the platform. He then put down my belongings and ran off. The train for East Grinstead came immediately, and I got on, wondering about this young man. Who was he? Where did he go? How did he know I wanted this particular train?" Esther concludes that she now trusts the Lord for everything because of the help she has received.

In 1986, Kerry Cole, a young housewife from Plymouth, had recently become the proud mother of a baby girl. "I was just getting to grips with new things like shopping with a carriage," she writes, "and was out with a friend. I stopped to look in a shop window, momentarily letting go of the carriage laden with shopping and the sleeping baby. You can imagine my extreme horror when I turned around to see my baby six inches away from rolling off the curb into three lanes of traffic."

With no pedestrians in sight, Kerry lunged toward the carriage, but was amazed to see a tall, brown-coated man suddenly appear right in front of the carriage, blocking its path. The first words on Kerry's lips were, "Oh, praise the Lord." The man gently replied, "Yes, indeed!" Kerry adds, "I can remember expecting some sharp rebuke for my carelessness, as you might expect from a passer-by, but his answer was warm and authoritative. I turned to my friend, for a moment, trembling with relief and joy. As I looked back, he just wasn't there anymore. I looked around me, but he had disappeared." Not surprisingly, Kerry is deeply grateful to God for the great love He showed toward a young learner mother and her baby.

Protection of a different kind was given to Audrey
Graham, a Christian in Newcastle, whose home area
had recently undergone a spate of burglaries. Some of
the neighbors were discussing the increasingly worry-
ing situation, when one of them surprised Audrey by
saying, "There is no need for *you* to worry." Puzzled,
Audrey asked why. The neighbor replied, "Every
night there are two giants guarding your flat. They
aren't from anywhere around here and they look so
big, I certainly wouldn't want to tangle with them!"
In Chapter 6 there is an account of two armored angels with swords protecting the home of another elderly lady in a troubled neigborhood, but in Audrey's
case they were giant-sized, human-looking angels.

An elderly lady called Irene Kevill, who is sometimes unsteady on her feet, had gone out of her back
door to put some trash in the garbage can. She hadn't
realized it was icy and became concerned that she
would fall. She seemed rooted to the spot, too frightened to attempt the return journey. Just then, a gentleman appeared from nowhere, took her arm and led
her safely back to the house. He disappeared, as silently as he had come, and Mrs. Kevill was convinced she had been helped by an angel.

Angels were the last thing on Kenneth Durlridge's
mind as he left work. For twenty-five years he had
always caught a bus on the main road and would wait
sitting on a low wall. On this occasion, when he
reached the bus stop, another man was already sitting
on the wall. They briefly acknowledged each other
and remarked on the weather. "After a while," says
Kenneth, "he rose and came to sit beside me. 'Tell
me,' he said, 'what is the most important thing in
your life?' I was thoroughly taken aback that a stranger should ask such a question. In the end I replied,

'I think the most important things in my life are my religious convictions.' He turned to look me full in the face and commented: 'That is a very good answer.' He then explained how much God loved me, and how important are the teachings of Jesus Christ."

Kenneth continues, "Just then the bus arrived, but the man stayed sitting on the wall. I got on the bus and turned to wave to him, but the wall was empty. There was no sign of him in any direction, nor on the bus." The man had simply vanished. Had Kenneth been speaking to an angel? He concludes: "One thing is sure; I shall never forget the man at the bus stop." Kenneth says, "I write to you only because it might help someone whose faith is as weak as mine was. My belief is that God works in mysterious ways. I offer no explanations for it except for its truth. At that time I was trying to relate Darwin's Theory of Evolution to the teachings of the Bible, and I had come to the end of my tether. At this point I decided to pray that God should reveal the 'truth' to me if it was His will." The result was the above encounter which convinced Kenneth of God's power shown through angels.

Angels come to bring God's Word to people and give witness to the Lord, but they do not preach. That task is entrusted to humans. In Daniel 9:20-7 the angel Gabriel appeared to Daniel while he was praying. He told Daniel what would happen in the future and gave testimony to the validity of the message from God which Daniel had seen in a vision.

During a very hot summer in the late 1960s Ray and Pam Fardon were leading a youth camp at Lee Abbey, near Lynton in North Devon. Just before lunch, Pam was appreciating the beauty of the coastline and noticed hundreds of people in the parking

lot, sitting by their cars eating their picnics. Suddenly
she heard the loud noise of an engine, and saw a tractor, out of control, careering wildly down a steep
field. The driver managed to steer it through the first
gate, but it was gaining speed at a frightening rate as
it hurtled down the second field. Many of the guests
at the house at the top of the hill and in the youth
camp watched with horror and prayed desperately for
the young man on the tractor to bring it under control, as it raced toward the crowds of holidaymakers.

Pam prayed, "Lord, please change its direction,"
and moments later it turned away from the parking
lot, banking on a small hillock. It missed the parking lot by yards and somersaulted over the cliff. Ray
took a few men with him and raced down the cliff
pathway, instructing everyone else to stay and pray. It
was time for lunch at the camp, but no one felt much
like eating.

Pam says, "All I could think of was that brave
young man desperately trying to steer the tractor to
safety. Eventually the men returned. 'He's dead, isn't
he?' I said to Ray. 'Who's dead?' he asked quietly.
'Well, the man in brown on the tractor.' He said, 'Tell
me what you saw.' I described the scene, finishing,
'It all happened so quickly; my last picture of him
was leaning right over the wheel, hands almost
crossed over.' My husband replied, 'There was no
one on the tractor.' 'But I saw him,' I said incredu-
lously. 'I saw him too,' Ray said, 'but we searched
the cliff face and everywhere and then news came
from the house. The tractor driver had left the engine
running while he went to shut the gate and he could
not get back in time. There was no one on it. The
tractor landed upside down on a car. The widowed
mother of a large family had been sitting in the car,

but she had just got out and walked to the chalet door, and was wondering why she had done so. The next moment the tractor came over the cliff and totally crushed her car. She was unharmed, as were the scores of people only yards away in the parking lot. There was no one on the tractor.'

"If that was so," writes Pam, "then who was the young man who had driven the tractor so brilliantly to the single place where its fall could be stopped by a one foot diameter oak tree and just one car, and, miraculously, no one be hurt?"

Further west, in Cornwall, Bob and Vi Code met an angel standing at the roadside in 1969. He didn't look like an angel but appeared to be a typical elderly Cornishman, with a waistcoat and fob watch. They were driving to Helston, when they saw him standing beside the road. He was not hitchhiking but they offered him a lift. He said he was going to Redruth, which was about six miles in the opposite direction. They were happy to take him there, even though it was a detour from their intended route.

Vi sat in the back, so that the man could be in the front. They did not have much conversation, although every now and then he said, "Praise the Lord." When they arrived in Redruth, Bob asked, "Where would you like to go?" The gentleman replied, "Just here will be fine"—and disappeared. The door had not opened and neither Bob driving nor Vi watching from the back seat saw where he went. It was so astonishing that neither of them felt like continuing their journey straight away. They decided instead to call on their friend, Bert Campbell, who lived in Redruth.

When Bert's wife opened the door to Bob and Vi she looked delighted to see them. She said, "We have been trying all day to get you on the phone, so as we couldn't contact you, we asked the Lord to bring you here. We urgently need a speaker for the Youth for Christ meeting this evening, and we would like Vi to talk about her experiences of God acting in her life." Suddenly it all made sense. The only reason they were meant to pick up that gentleman was to divert them to Redruth. He had been standing on the wrong side of the road to catch a bus to Redruth, but Bob and Vi would not have stopped to offer him assistance if he had been waiting in the right place. The Campbells and Codes praised the Lord for His intervention that day.

It is common conviction among Christians that God has the prerogative to intervene in every individual's life, to rescue and give help. In these reported appearances, it seems He chose to send angels to give assistance, although they appeared in human form.

# CHAPTER FIVE

# *Traditional Angels*

bout half the people who have told me of their angel experience have seen a traditional-looking angel: tradition in the sense of the Bible's description of them. Usually the Biblical appearances are mentioned in an entirely matter-of-fact way, for example, "an angel of the Lord came to them" or "an angel from heaven appeared to him." Perhaps they were so accepted that descriptions were superfluous! However, the Bible does give us some clues by describing the actions of the angels such as standing (Luke 1:11), walking (Acts 12:9), shaking Peter on the shoulder to wake him up (Acts 12:7), calling out (Genesis 22:11), guiding the people of Israel through the desert (Exodus 14:19), holding a sword (Numbers 22:23), praising God (Luke 2:13), feeding Jesus (Matthew 4:11), opening the doors of a jail (Acts 5:19), shutting the mouths of lions (Daniel 6:22), and speaking to people (Matthew 28:5).

The largest collection of accounts of angelic activity is found in the Book of Revelation, the last book of the Bible. These include blowing trumpets (Revelation 8:7), swinging a sickle (14:19), holding a scroll (10:8), carrying a key and heavy chain (20:1), flying high in the air (14:6), measuring a wall (21:15), standing on the sea (10:5) and picking up a stone the size of a millstone (18:21).

Elsewhere, angels are described as being "two angels in white" (John 20:12), and "two men dressed in white" (Acts 1:10). One of the fullest descriptions is found in Matthew's account of the Resurrection of Jesus (28:2-4), which I quote in full. "There was a violent earthquake for an angel of the Lord came down from heaven and going to the tomb rolled back the stone and sat on it. His appearance was like lightning, and his clothes were white as snow. The guards were so afraid that they shook and became like dead men."

Another similarly dramatic description is found in Revelations 10:1: "I saw another mighty angel coming down from heaven. He was robed in a cloud, with a rainbow above his head; his face was like the sun, and his legs were like fiery pillars."

Some of the people who have described their experience of seeing an angel speak of dazzling brightness and an overwhelming sense of peace. Ralph Bellamy, who lives in Highcliffe, Dorset, tells of an incident which happened to his late wife, Joan, in August 1940. At the time, they were living in a bungalow on the fringe of the RAF Kenley aerodrome. This was considered a danger zone, as Hitler's intention was to destroy the fighter stations. One day, while her husband was at work, there was a morning air raid. While the sirens sounded, Joan quickly made her way to the Anderson shelter in the garden. Ralph writes: "The bombs started dropping all around and she was petrified. She prayed to the Lord for help and an angel appeared in dazzling white and stood at the entrance of the shelter. Joan held out her hand; she and the angel held hands while the air raid was in progress. The bombs were still dropping and dust was rising from the ground, but Joan was at perfect peace in the presence of the angel. The All Clear sounded and the angel vanished. After this Joan always referred to her 'guardian angel.' "

Angels come to the aid of humans for many different reasons. Joan Bellamy received courage and protection during the air raid. Diana Matthews was feeling similarly vulnerable about two years ago when she saw an angel. Her husband, the curate at Great Baddow, Essex, had to be away from home for a few days. This left Diana, who was pregnant, to look after their young daughter, Hannah, alone. The back garden fence had been broken so there was no protection from the public footpath, which contributed toward Diana's feelings of vulnerability. As she prayed she saw an angel sitting on the gate post at the end of the garden. He looked so strong that she felt reassured and she thanked God for His protection of her and Hannah.

Irene Pole was also feeling in need of protection when she had her angel experience. As one of ten children there were always others around, so she was never alone. When she married, Irene and her husband lived in a terraced house near the family but, on retiring, they moved to a detached bungalow in Leicester, which has a spacious hall with six rooms leading off it. Soon after they moved in, about ten years ago, Irene found herself alone for the first time in her life, and it terrified her. She prayed for help and immediately the hall where she was standing appeared to be full of angels. They were moving around effort-

lessly, wearing long robes. She saw that their faces
were kindly and caring, which made her feel comforted and peaceful. The fear has never returned as
this incident made her realize the nearness and power
of God. Irene says it reminded her of the time in the
Book of Kings where Elisha was unperturbed by the
large number of enemies around them, but his servant
was terrified. Elisha prayed, "O Lord, open his eyes
so that he may see" (2 Kings 6:17). At once, the servant was able to see "the hills full of horses and chariots of fire all round Elisha," far more in number than
the enemy and he knew God would protect them.

On several occasions angels have appeared to as-
sist the dying. Dora Deighton, who lives on the Isle
of Wight, wrote to tell me about the moment of her
mother-in-law's death. She says: "I had looked after
her for several months and I loved her very much.
When she died I walked across the room to open the
window and I saw two big angels. One had his left
wing laid over the other one's right wing, and lying
on their wings was my mother-in-law, who had just
died. They very gently carried her away. I didn't cry,
I felt so happy for her."

Averil Gilder was also present at the peaceful
death of her mother in June 1948 near Bognor, Sussex. She and her sister Peggy had sat up all night at
their mother's bedside. Peggy had gone out to the
kitchen to make some tea, while Averil stayed with
her mother. She reports: "Suddenly a *brilliant* light
shone from the other end of her bed. There was no
window there. I saw a floating figure, the head and
wings being the clearest features. Mother sat up and
reached out toward the angel. It didn't last more than
a minute or two. Then the light faded and seemed to
float away. Mother sank back on her pillows. She

went at that moment; she had followed the angel. I feel quite sure about that."

Angels have also been known to give comfort to the bereaved, as in the case of Harry Knight. The wife of Harry's brother had just died, only hours after being taken ill. His brother had two young children and was broken-hearted with grief. Harry stayed with him and, after a sleepless night, the two of them knelt by the settee, Harry making a desperate, urgent appeal to God for help. As they prayed, Harry was aware of a third person of about their size floating on the left of them. Harry knows this was an angel and he concludes: "The result was remarkable help and clear guidance for the family as the angel showed God's loving control in the situation."

The encouragement Susan Clegg received from an angel experience was not just for herself but for the whole church she attends in Birmingham. As she parked near the church one Sunday evening, Susan noticed a strange light above the roof. "Looking up," she says, "I saw two angels about two or three feet above the roof of St. John's. They had the appearance of men, but the head area was dazzlingly bright. They wore long, white robes and each carried a brilliant sword which was pointed down toward the roof as if at rest. It felt a bit scary, so I prayed for God's protection in the spiritual battle. As I did so, the angels raised their swords and looked 'at the ready.' " Needless to say, the sense of God's presence was especially real for her during the service that evening.

Many of the people who have written to me have spoken of the reassurance they have felt after seeing an angel. In 1983, Ryder Rogers, a Baptist minister, was taking a group to a Girls' Brigade camp in North Devon. After the journey, he was lying on the grass praying about the camp, when he saw four angels at the corners of the camp. As a result, he felt secure in the knowledge that the girls would be safe.

A whole ring of angels with swords was seen protecting a large group of children at Peterborough Bible Week in May 1989. Carl Richards was the drummer in the music group. During the worship, as "the children were singing their little hearts out I saw many angels standing shoulder to shoulder right around the hall, facing inward to where we were all seated. They were solid figures all above seven feet tall, glowing very brightly, especially the eyes which were obscured by the intensity of the light."

The angels Carl saw wore "simple wrap-around robes tied at the waist. Their hair was shoulder-length, light-colored and wavy. In their hands they each held a long two-edged sword which they leaned upon. Behind their backs there were two huge folded wings. Their feet were not visible to me; it was as though their legs faded at the bottom. They were whispering to each other, and occasionally smilingly pointed out certain children. I would describe them as being in a state of great excitement as they were constantly fidgeting and their wings were trembling. I was able to watch them for about five minutes until they slowly faded from view." Carl was thrilled to see them for so long, aware that they were there for the children's protection. He concludes, "I can assure you that all this is accurate, as immediately after the event I penned what had happened and, being an artist, I also drew what I had seen. As you can imagine I felt completely awestruck while this was going on, and after the meeting I had to take a quiet walk to muse on what I had seen and to praise my Lord for allowing me to see this."

On other occasions God shows His protection for just one person, not a group. Alison Pike, aged eight, was walking to school on her own for the first time, as previously her mother had walked with her. That morning her mother, Sandra, had prayed that the Lord would keep Alison safe. As she walked down the drive, Sandra saw an angel walking beside Alison, watching over her. She had not expected to see any physical sign of God's safe-keeping. When she later told Alison that she had seen an angel, Alison was overjoyed.

In 1990, Barbara Whiting's eight-year-old daughter, Philippa, needed to be looked after by friends while her mother was working. One day, after school, she was to go to the friends' home near where they live in Farnham. As usual, Barbara prayed for God's protection for Philippa, and saw a picture of an angel looking after her daughter. Barbara says, "The angel was enormous, much bigger than a man, but it was the wings which left such a vivid impression: powerful, so big and yet the feathers so white and gentle somehow. I was reminded of God's promise in Psalm 91:4, 'He will cover you with His feathers, and under His wings you will find refuge.' This is very special for me."

Janet Hathaway, an English graduate who teaches in a comprehensive school in Bolton, on the edge of the Pennines, saw angels during the school carol service on December 12, 1991. During the service she was praising God silently, when she looked up and saw six angels in the pine open-timbered roof of the church. Janet describes what she saw: "There were four in the middle and two at the front of the nave, all facing inward. In form, they resembled the whitish quality of figures etched on glass. The two at the

front were blowing trumpets, although I did not hear
them. These winged figures were fine, gentle, grace-
ful and ethereal. Although I saw them for a short
time only, I knew that God was telling me that they
were with us throughout. A few weeks later I told our
Jewish headmaster and said I believed they were a
sign of God's protection and an affirmation that He
was pleased with what we were doing."

In the Bible, angels appeared several times to people who needed to be given a message or helped in
some way. Often, the circumstances and words are
given more importance than the angels' appearance.
Acts 10:3, for example, describes how Cornelius, a
Roman centurion, encountered God's reality: "One
day at about three in the afternoon he had a vision.
He distinctly saw an angel of God, who came to him
and said, 'Cornelius!' " The angel told him to send
for Peter to explain to him the truth about God. The
angel gave precise instructions about where to find
Peter, who Cornelius did not know. "Send men to
Joppa to bring back a man named Simon who is
called Peter. He is staying with Simon the tanner
whose house is by the sea." The men sent by
Cornelius had no trouble in finding Peter.

The angel's message to Cornelius was instantly
obeyed. Similarly, Vicki Stafford of Crowborough,
Sussex, was left in no doubt that she should obey the
angelic message given to her. At the time, she was
awake in bed at 2 A.M., suffering from an asthma attack, and had got out of bed to open the window to
try a change of air. Her ground-floor bedroom looks
out on to the back garden, and she immediately noticed a young man on the lawn. At first she thought
he was the intruder who had been attacking women
in the area and, not being a nervous sort, she decided

to confront him to frighten him off. As she opened
the window to call to him, she saw that what she had
thought was a short fair youth was actually a tall angel, kneeling as if in prayer. Vicki says, "He was half
turned away from me, with wings, looking as if he
had stepped off an ornate tomb! My first reaction was
utter amazement, my second was feeling like an intruder myself, seeing something totally private. I
watched him silently for a while, then closed the window as quietly as I could and got back into bed."

Vicki relates the surprising sequel: "I lay there
thinking, 'Some people have gnomes in their gardens,
I've got an angel in mine!' I felt a weird mixture of
pleasure, 'This is ridiculous' and 'Have I lost my
marbles?' and then the angel spoke to me. I was
aware of his message as an emerging consciousness.
He told me not to be judgmental of people, even
when I was sure they were wrong; that only God may
judge. Not to hate people for what they do, but to understand. That life on earth is only a tiny droplet in
the ocean of eternity and my concern should be to try
to become as close to God as I could, since God is
composed of love and light. Really, I don't have
words to describe his message. I can only say I was
filled with an incredible sense of love and knew I
was feeling heaven. Written down, the message
sounds simplistic, yet it was full of subtlety; he spoke
to my understanding. I fell asleep filled with enlight-
enment. For some time I felt burned out, scorched; it
took several weeks to realize the full effect. The angel had taken my anger and left me with self-
knowledge and illumination. Those who know me
well comment on a change; I am a richer, more committed and gentler person as a result."

Raymond Mallitte of Leyton, East London, asked

God that someone else should be blessed by an angel.
He had been greatly helped by the elderly couple
next door, during and after his stay in the hospital.
Raymond wanted to thank them, so he prayed that
God would send one of His angels to bless them. He
then began to wonder how he would know if the
prayer had been answered, so he prayed again asking
to know that his prayers had been heard. Raymond
takes up the story: "My neighbors invited me in for
a cup of tea, a most unusual occurrence. The wife
told me that a few days earlier she had been in the
front room when suddenly it felt extremely peaceful.
Out of the corner of her eye she had seen a man
dressed all in gold, standing in the corner of the
room, making the sign of the cross. She said it was
a beautiful experience, especially the sense of peace
which permeated the room. I knew that God had answered my prayers."

An incident which was totally unbidden happened
in the home of an elderly lady, Mrs. Mereet, who
each week hosted a prayer meeting in her front room.
Many people became Christians in that room and
were blessed by the peace and sense of God's presence there. One evening the prayer meeting had gone
on very late, so when everyone went home Mrs.
Mereet went straight to bed and slept soundly. The
next morning, when she came downstairs, she saw a
light shining from under the front room door. "Oh,
my goodness," she thought, "I must have left the
light on." She pushed open the door and stood trans-
fixed. There on the rug in front of the fireplace stood
an angel in shining white robes. He smiled at her and
then he disappeared before her eyes, leaving the room
in darkness. Mrs. Mereet was thrilled; all she could
say was "Thank you, Jesus." She was eighty-five at

the time, but her meetings continued to be blessed until she went to be with her Lord at the age of eighty-nine.

Joyce Davey, a trained nurse living in Braunton, Devon, was worried about her husband who was seriously ill with heart and breathing problems. After a terrible night on May 10, 1969, the doctor came and warned Joyce that her husband was most unlikely to recover. Joyce, however, clung to a promise from the Lord back in February, when her husband had first become ill, that he would make a good recovery. At bedtime, Joyce made her husband as comfortable as possible, although his gasping for breath meant he had to sleep sitting up. Joyce describes what happened next: "Just then angels started to surround our bungalow, shadowy figures, all facing inward. There were so many I could not possibly count them. The 'chief one' came and insisted I went to sleep; no harm would come while they were there. I slept amazingly well, waking only once to attend to my husband. At eight o'clock the following morning, I was literally shaken from my sleep and, as I opened my eyes, the last few angels were departing. The 'chief one' was by me saying, 'Hurry up, we have to go, all is well,' and he was gone. I sat up and could hardly believe how peaceful my husband looked. He was pink and lying down, breathing easily, instead of blue and gasping. When the doctor saw him, he couldn't speak for amazement." Some time later the doctor said to Joyce, "Medically that was an impossibility. It was only your prayers and faith that saved him." Joyce then told him about the angels. Her husband continued to make excellent progress.

All of us remember some things more clearly than others, even from years ago. Those who have been privileged to see an angel, wings and all, can recall the scene in vivid detail. They find the experience awe-inspiring and are left in no doubt that the visitor was directly from God.

# CHAPTER SIX

# Cherub, Seraph and Archangel

he Bible refers to angelic beings in thirty-four of its sixty-six books, and describes different kinds whose appearances match their various roles. Angels are most frequently mentioned, but there are also several references to cherubim. Archangels appear only twice and seraphim are described in detail only once.

Only one angel, Gabriel, and one archangel, Michael, are referred to by name in the Bible, although the angel Raphael and the archangel Jeremiel are also named in the Apocrypha. Gabriel appeared to Daniel, to explain the meaning of a vision (Daniel 9:21); to Zechariah, giving him the news of a son, who became John the Baptist (Luke 1:19); and to Mary, telling her that she would be the mother of Jesus (Luke 1:26). Michael the archangel is named in Jude 9 and seems to hold more authority than ordinary angels, who are simply messengers. The archangel Michael is described as "disputing with the devil" and he appears to have an important role in the fight against evil.

Seven people have seen an angel they identified as the archangel Michael but two were both involved in prayer against evil or controlling forces at the time. Jill Rainey of Wimborne had been discussing with a friend the importance of giving up to the Lord the negative and evil influences which had shaped and affected their lives up to the present. They realized that prayer is sometimes necessary specifically to "cut someone loose" from the past and set them free to become the person they should be. Later, in her bedroom, Jill asked the Lord about this possibility. She explains, "Suddenly there was at my left side a figure about nine feet tall, holding a very long gleaming sword. He brought it down swiftly in a cutting action towards my feet. This quick movement was most dramatic. I have never again doubted the necessity of being cut free from the past and have shared this with others when praying for their healing."

Sheila Richards from Cornwall told me about two friends who were walking in an area where many children were known to have been abused and murdered and not had any funeral. As they walked along a narrow pathway, they committed these murdered children to the Lord's safe keeping and sprinkled holy water for cleansing. Suddenly they were aware of someone behind them and turned to see a huge figure, nine or ten feet tall—they did not dare to look at his face because they were so overawed. He was clothed in gold and white, with an enormous sword held at waist height. The blade was pointing upward with tongues of fire from top to bottom on both sides. It was a brilliant, powerful light, almost too bright to look at. They knew this was a sign that nothing in opposition to God would be allowed to pass along that path again. They were both certain they had seen the archangel Michael.

In another instance, the assistant priest at Glastonbury church had always felt a sense of foreboding every time he approached Glastonbury, even though he had lived and worked there for three years. In a prayer group, the vicar's wife, Elizabeth Riley, saw the archangel Michael standing above the assistant. When she told him, he found immediate and lasting encouragement as he felt the visit of the archangel somehow redeemed Glastonbury for him. Although evil or controlling forces were not involved, his sense of foreboding was perhaps connected with the pagan and more recent New Age practices for which Glastonbury is now well known.

Beatrice Collins was attending a Holy Communion service at a church in Bournemouth on Whitsunday 1982. As she was listening to the sermon, she became aware of a gigantic angelic figure towering above the preacher. She says, "This dazzling figure, who I recognized as the archangel Michael, was clothed in brilliant scintillating light, filling all the space on the brick wall behind the pulpit right up to the roof. I gazed at the awe-inspiring sight for a few minutes until it slowly faded away. This will forever live in my memory as a never to be forgotten experience."

Cherubim, the second most frequently mentioned category of angelic being in the Bible, are the strong guards used by God to enforce His word. "After He drove the man [Adam] out, He placed on the east side of the Garden of Eden cherubim and a flaming sword flashing back and forth to guard the way to the tree of life" (Genesis 3:24). King David sang the praises

of the Lord, thanking Him for delivering him from
the hands of his enemies. He says, "The Lord is my
rock, my fortress and my deliverer; . . . He mounted
the cherubim and flew; He soared on the wings of the
wind." God is praised in this way in 2 Samuel 22:11
and in Psalm 18:10 and in this context the cherubim
are seen assisting the Lord in His actions.

In his lengthy vision, the prophet Ezekiel saw the
coming destruction of Jerusalem because of the wicked-
ness of God's chosen people. He also saw "the glory of
the Lord" and "an immense cloud with flashing lightning and surrounded by brilliant light . . . in the fire
was what looked like four living creatures. They had
two wings outstretched and two wings covering the
body. Beside each was a wheel which could move in
any direction without turning, each was like a wheel in-
tersecting a wheel." The four living creatures could
move speedily, in any direction, and "their appearance
was like burning coals of fire. Fire moved among the
creatures; it was bright with lightning flashing out of
it." Ezekiel says, "When the creatures moved, I heard
the sound of their wings, like the voice of the Almighty. When they stood still they lowered their
wings . . . Above the expanse over their heads was
what looked like a throne of sapphire, and high above
on the throne was a figure like that of a man . . . and
brilliant light surrounded him. This was the appearance
of the likeness of the glory of the Lord. When I saw it,
I fell face down" (Ezekiel 1:4-28).

Later in Ezekiel, chapters 9 and 10, these "living
creatures" of Chapter 1 are called cherubim. Ezekiel
says,

*Now the glory of the Lord went up from above
the cherubim, where it had been . . . I looked*

*and saw the likeness of a throne of sapphire
above the expanse that was over the heads of
the cherubim. The Lord said to the man clothed
in linen, "Go in among the wheels beneath the
cherubim. Fill your hands with burning coals
from among the cherubim and scatter them over
the city." ... The cloud filled the temple, and
the court was full of the radiance of the glory
of the Lord. The sound of the wings of the cherubim could be heard as far away as the outer
court, like the voice of God Almighty when He
speaks ... Each of the cherubim had four faces:
one face was that of a cherub, the second the
face of a man, the third the face of a lion, and
the fourth the face of an eagle. Then the cherubim rose upward ... These were the living creatures I had seen beneath the God of Israel by
the Kebar River, and I realized that they were
cherubim.*

Ezekiel's descriptions are very detailed so he must
have experienced these visions very clearly. He had a
tremendous sense of God's holiness and, while living
in exile in Babylonia, he felt deeply the judgment for
sin that would fall on Jerusalem. Similar living creatures are also described in detail in the Book of Revelation, when John was privileged to see a vision of
heaven. These had six wings each and many eyes,
and they are continually worshiping God, encircling
His throne.

During Pentecost 1991, a team led by Barry
Kissell was ministering at a church, again in Glastonbury. When the church leaders and the team were all
praying in "the upper room" Elizabeth Riley saw two
cherub angels fly into the room and remain by Bar-

ry's right shoulder. He did not see them himself, but
Elizabeth knew they were strengthening him as he
prepared to preach and lead the team.

The other cherubim we read much about in the Bible are those portrayed in wood and gold in the Temple and on the precious ark of the Covenant. This ark,
also called the ark of the Testimony, was a chest
made of acacia wood, about three feet long. It was
overlaid with pure gold and had a cover above it,
called an atonement cover. On each end of the cover
was a cherub made out of hammered gold, of one
piece with the cover. They faced each other with their
wings spread upward, overshadowing the cover with
them. Unlike those seen by Ezekiel, these cherubim
each had one face and two wings. The ark of the Testimony contained the tablets of stone inscribed with
the Ten Commandments God gave to His people.
They carried the ark with them when they were traveling through the wilderness, as it symbolized to
them God's presence. The Lord said to Moses,
"Above the cover between the two cherubim that are
over the ark of the Testimony, I will meet with you
and give you all My commands for the Israelites"
(Exodus 25:22). The ark of the Testimony was kept
in the Tabernacle, which was a movable tent used by
the Israelites while they had no permanent home.
This was the meeting place where the people gathered to worship God. Even the curtains of the Tabernacle had cherubim worked into them by skilled
craftsmen.

Once the Israelites were settled in the land of Israel, Solomon built an elaborate Temple, which also
featured cherubim. These were 15 feet high and 15
feet across, from the tips of their outstretched wings,
sheltering the ark of the Testimony. Solomon "placed

the cherubim inside the innermost room of the Temple with their wings spread out." They were made of olive wood, overlaid with pure gold. Again, these cherubim had one face and two wings each. These are the kind of cherub which have been seen by people today. Maybe the more holy variety, of Ezekiel's vision, remain in heaven so are not seen on earth.

Several people have described the angel they have seen as being like "a cherub." Roberta Bowman was studying at the University of the West Indies in Trinidad and was praying for David, a colleague on the campus, who was terminally ill with cancer. Roberta had arranged a gathering to pray for his healing, so David, his parents and his Roman Catholic priest were together praying in Roberta's room. Roberta says, "A cherub flew into the room, and my immediate reaction was to prostrate myself on my face. The room was filled with peace and it was an electrifying experience. I never thought a cherub was real, just on Christmas cards, but they are very real. The awesome presence of God filled the place. It was a tremendously beautiful and awe-inspiring experience."

Another sighting of cherubim was by Rhiain Stafford, of Nether Stowey, Somerset. She has had two experiences of seeing angels, but as both occurred in the same year, she was able to distinguish between seeing angels and cherubim. In the first instance, on May 12, 1991, she was attending an open-air service of worship in the Blackdown Hills. During a time of worshipful singing, Rhiain looked up and saw "a cloud of angels" also singing. She says, "It was a quite amazing sight, and I felt they were protecting us." On August 16, she was at the Communion service on the last day of New Wine, the Christian summer camp in Somerset. During the worship time,

Rhiain saw cherubim among the rafters of the huge auditorium. They were joining in the worship and playing long trumpets, as in Revelation 8:6. Two months later Rhiain developed a severe form of leukaemia, from which she has been healed, so perhaps the thrilling sight of the angels encouraged her faith during this illness.

Pauline Hannaby of Cheltenham has also been fortunate enough to see angels more than once. In 1971 she saw a tall, powerful angel, standing in a doorway, and although she could see every detail of him clearly, he was also transparent so she could see the background through him. This experience came after Pauline had been asking the Lord to show her the invisible world which surrounds us. Almost twenty years later, in 1990, she again saw angelic beings, but this time they were completely different. Because she was feeling particularly sad following her husband's death, she prayed before going to sleep, expressing her feelings to God. During the night she awoke and the room was pitch black as usual. Then she saw the ceiling become covered with dozens of happy winged figures. Pauline describes them: "They all looked so animated, excitedly chattering to each other, not looking at me. There were so many of them, behind one another, that all I could see were heads, shoulders, and wings. They were in pairs, each pair having a different pose, some full face, some in profile. Their wings were white with brown tips and their hair was curly. As I watched them, the Lord said to me, 'The angel of My presence watches over you.' I was very tired and eventually had to close my eyes, even though I fought against it. When I opened my eyes again, the ceiling was completely dark. I have never seen that lovely, comforting sight again."

Seraphim are described only in Isaiah 6, when Isaiah the prophet had a vision of the holy Lord in heaven:

*I saw the Lord seated on a throne, high and exalted, and the train of His robe filled the temple. Above Him were seraphs, each with six wings. With two wings they covered their faces, with two they covered their feet and with two they were flying. And they were calling to one another:*

*"Holy, holy, holy is the Lord Almighty; the whole earth is full of His glory."*

Isaiah's vision continued:

*At the sound of their voices the doorposts and thresholds shook and the temple was filled with smoke. "Woe to me," I cried, "I am ruined! For I am a man of unclean lips, and I live among a people of unclean lips, and my eyes have seen the King, the Lord Almighty." Then one of the seraphs flew to me with a live coal in his hand, which he had taken with tongs from the altar. With it he touched my mouth and said, "See, this has touched your lips, your guilt is taken away and your sin atoned for." Then I heard the voice of the Lord saying, "Whom shall I send? And who will go for us?" And I said, "Here I am. Send me!"*

The Lord then told Isaiah all that he was to tell His people.

Seraphim means "burning ones" from the word *saraph*—to burn. These six-winged beings are also described in Revelation as being around the throne of God in the vision the apostle John saw of heaven. Isaiah and John must have been especially privileged to see the seraphim. They are very close to the throne of God, so presumably they are not sent to earth to help humans. This would explain why six-winged beings have not been described by those telling me of angel experiences, although some people have described visions similar to those of Isaiah and John, which they have had while praying.

About forty years ago, for example, Norah de la Mare Norris was distressed as her home was due to be demolished. She was kneeling in her sitting room, praying about what she should do, when she suddenly felt herself being lifted upward, although she was alone and unaware of anyone holding her. Norah says, "I was at the gate of heaven, and angels were clustering all round the gate, all white and golden and full of movement. They were playing instruments and singing; the music was wonderful. I couldn't tell how long it lasted, then all at once I was back on the floor, trembling all over. I felt so sorry I was still there with life to be lived and troubles to be surmounted, yet I had the wonderful certainty to carry through the rest of my life, that God is in heaven with His ministering angels. I am a terribly ordinary woman and yet even such a poor thing as I has been blessed with a taste of the marvels God has prepared for those who love Him. I felt a 'trembling joy' for about two weeks, following this vision. It happened when I was aged about forty, and it strengthened my certainty that angels are constantly with God in heaven. I have shared it with only a few special friends because it is too precious to be the object of scorn, but I have written it now so that others may feel more conscious of the presence of God's angels today."

Norah did not have what is commonly called an "out of body" or "near death" experience. That can happen when someone has been seriously injured or is very ill. They may "die" for a while and apparently leave their body, but are then revived by medical intervention. This was not Norah's experience, nor that of the two cases following, since they were all perfectly well, wide awake and in their right mind at the time.

Cicely Dyer was returning from work at a guesthouse near Taunton. Her boss had been very upset, as her vicar had just died. Cicely felt that she had given a very inadequate reply to someone newly bereaved, particularly as it was not long since her own son had died. She prayed before setting off on her moped that God would help her to know what to say to other bereaved people. On the journey home, approaching a bend in the road, Cicely says, "I was suddenly uplifted and saw through the clouds a vision of angels singing and swaying with delight because this Christian vicar had now gone to heaven. The scene was excruciatingly beautiful, with delicate pastel colors. I took in all the detail, but it must have lasted only a split second in our time, because I came back to earth, still on my moped approaching the same bend in the road." Luke 15:10 states, "There is rejoicing in the presence of the angels of God over one sinner who repents."

In March 1987 Janet Harrison of Buckingham was praying to the Lord when she, too, saw a wonderful vision of heaven. She says, "I was in the temple and at the far end sat Jesus on His throne at the top of a staircase. His robe fell like a train down one side of

the steps. Down the other side of the steps water
flowed like a stream. All around, above and on both
sides were angels and light, making an arch of angel
wings above Him. Jesus looked at me and through
me, as if He were reading me. I knew He wanted me
to speak for Him, but I was making excuses—'I am
not eloquent; I always put my big foot in it; I'm
afraid.' Then Jesus touched my lips, which tingled at
the touch of His hand, and He spoke to me: 'Go in
My Name, empowered by My Spirit; do not be
afraid, I am with you.' I knew He was commissioning me to do what He asked me to do. This involved
the gift of prophecy, which until then had been just to
give words of encouragement to others. Recently it
had been becoming uncomfortable, as I had been
given instructions and warnings to give to church
people from the Lord, but I had been reluctant to pass
them on to the relevant people. I also knew He
wanted me to speak at meetings, which has gradually
increased over the years, although I felt very timid
before this dramatic commissioning."

The experience Janet had bears a resemblance to
Moses' commissioning when the angel of the Lord
appeared to him in a burning bush which was not
consumed by fire (Exodus 3:2). Then God Himself
spoke to Moses, telling him to go and plead for Phar-
aoh, the ruler of Egypt, to release the people of Israel
from slavery. Moses made excuses of lack of ability
and eloquence, just like Janet had done when confronted by a challenging commission from the Lord.

When "the angel of the Lord" is mentioned in the
Old Testament, it may refer to a particularly mighty
angel or even the Messiah, taking the form of an angel so that He could appear in person. In Jewish
teaching "the angel of the Lord" is called Metatron,

which means "the angel of countenance" because he reveals an aspect of the face of God. In 1 Chronicles 21, King David saw "the angel of the Lord standing between heaven and earth with a drawn sword in his hand, extended over Jerusalem." It is recorded that at least five other people saw the angel too, and were in awe of him. Several people have reported seeing an angel wielding a powerful sword, giving them protection. Janet Harrison also had an experience of this sort. One evening she prayed for protection of her home since her husband was away and there had been a number of break-ins in the area. Looking out of the window before going to bed, Janet saw "a huge angel on the drive; he shone brightly and he held in his hand a mighty drawn sword, which also shone. He wore a long robe and I felt very aware of his protection."

In 1989 the Derbyshire street where Mrs. Dorothy Forster had always lived had become overrun by drug-users and pushers and it was not safe for the elderly to go out in the evenings. Feeling anxious one evening, she decided to leave the landing light on, then heard the Lord speak to her: "Can't you trust Me, my child?" She replied, "Of course I trust You, Lord," and went to switch off the light. She explains, "Then I could see, just outside my front door, two warrior angels in full armor from head to toe, including big iron helmets. They were about ten feet tall, one each side of my door, each holding a long spear which they crossed over my door. I said to the Lord, 'If anyone tries to break in, Lord, they would be terrified and run!' I now know that those warrior angels are always there." This is the protection promised to believers in Psalm 34:7, "The angel of the Lord en-

camps around those who fear Him, and He delivers
them."

Over the centuries the idea has developed of a personal guardian angel for each person, constantly on
one's shoulder. In the *New Catholic Encyclopedia*
T. L. Fallon writes, "The concept of guardian angel
as a distinct spiritual being sent by God to protect every individual man is a development of Catholic theology and piety, not literally contained in the Bible,
but fostered by it." It is true that "He will command
His angels concerning you to guard you in all your
ways" (Psalm 91:11), but that protection is carried
out immediately, each time assistance is required.
Angels can travel any distance in a split second, and
any number can be sent to protect us, not just one.
Some people have seen four angels, or several, arriving to help them, the number varying according to
the severity of the situation. Angels spend most of
their time in heaven. Speaking of children, Jesus said,
"Their angels in heaven always see the face of my
Father" (Matthew 18:10). They respond instantly to
His commands to visit earth to rescue someone in
danger, but the rest of the time they are looking at
God's face, not hovering at our elbow. This protection is not just for children, but is continued throughout our lives, as is evidenced in the many examples
given in this book.

When Ted and Beryl Sisley returned to their home
in Wisbech, Cambridgeshire, one evening in 1979, a
rough-looking group of travelers had taken up resi-
dence uninvited at the end of their garden. Beryl explains, "The dogs were all barking and the leader of
the group seemed to be in a great state of fear. What
seemed to terrify him most was seeing a tall man
dressed in white standing by our kitchen door! They

were off early the next morning, lock, stock and barrel. I wondered if the traveler thought he would take a look in our house while we were absent, but God's angel had prevented him."

Margaret Foinette of Falkirk, Scotland, was exhausted from looking after her 90-year-old mother, who was suffering from Alzheimer's disease. In June 1987, two friends went with Margaret to the doctor to plead for her mother to be taken into the hospital, but unfortunately there were no beds available. Later that morning, back at Margaret's home, the three ladies prayed together about the situation. The Lord brought to mind the miraculous arrival of the White Cavalry, during World War I, at La Bassée (see page 112). Margaret found the account of this angelic intervention in a book and read it to her friends. They prayed again and the two friends went home.

What happened next was a tremendous encouragement to Margaret, as she explains: "All that afternoon I watched a column of white cavalry ride on to 'my battlefield' but there was no leader. They gathered round in a circle and raised a standard. I expected them to leave after a while, but they did not—this was an army of occupation. All that week I continued to nurse my mother, greatly appreciating the supernatural help the Lord was giving me. During that time, I looked out the window and saw an angel standing on the pavement outside. He was the leader, in a military uniform, with steel helmet and breastplate, and no wings. All his clothing and equipment were exquisitely beautiful, of an iridescent pale green. The breastplate was made of small plates like overlapping scales, and he just stood there on guard. He was of tremendous stature; my rooms are over ten feet high, but he was considerably taller. I have told

several people about my angel-on-guard and two others have said they have also seen them."

Similar protection, though on a smaller scale, was
given to Ruth Rushman in London in 1990, as she
was feeling very low and in need of encouragement.
Praying to God alone in her bedroom, she asked to be
allowed to see an angel. Immediately one appeared
before her, powerful and awe-inspiring. She felt overwhelmed at the sight and humbled that such a privilege had been granted to her. Grace Matthews of
Byfleet, Surrey, was also feeling vulnerable in 1938
as she was almost nine months' pregnant and was
alone at home while her husband was on night duty.
Just before getting into bed she looked out of the
bedroom window and was thrilled to see the beautiful
figure of an angel, high in the sky.

Madeleine Darby runs a Christian bookshop in
Wigan with her husband. One night, in 1991, she was
on her own with three young children and one-on-
the-way, as her husband was away at a three-day conference. Feeling lonely, she slept downstairs in the
living room with the light on. She woke up suddenly
at 10:30 P.M. and saw an angel standing at the side of
the living room. He was about eight feet tall, strong-
looking, with broad shoulders and a wide chin.
Madeleine says, "Inwardly I thanked God for His reassurance of safety, smiled and dozed off to sleep. At
2:15 A.M. I woke again, to find the same angel still
there and another one at the opposite side of the
room. This one was a few inches shorter and looked
more youthful. They both seemed 'on guard' and
were clothed in white. The first had shoulder-length
hair, that of the second was more wavy. Both had
long swords at their left sides, and seemed to have
wings behind their wide shoulders. I know this must

sound unbelievable, but I knew from that moment never to doubt God's protection."

Sometimes a joint concern shared by several people praying together may be encouraged by one or more of them seeing an angel. On October 9, 1977, Jessie Dickinson, who now lives in Wolverhampton, was at a Quaker meeting for worship. All shared news of friends and neighbors who were ill, some terminally. Then Barbara, the treasurer, prayed aloud for all those mentioned. Jessie felt "a wonderful sense of love and power enfolding us all. After a time, I noticed two people standing in front of Barbara. One was slightly taller than the other and both wore long yellow-golden robes. I was puzzling as to why I couldn't see their arms, when I suddenly realized it was because of their wings, which were folded down. Wings! This brought me up with a jerk, as I recognized that the two I had been studying so calmly were angels. As I continued to gaze at them, the two figures gradually became silvery and faded away. I stammered, 'I have just seen two angels standing in front of Barbara.' The power and wonder of this unbelievable experience have remained with me ever since; nothing can ever take it away from me."

In 1991 Betty Marshall, one of the elders at Buckhurst Hill Baptist Church was praying with the other elders about whether the man they were considering to invite as their new minister was the right choice. As they were praying, Betty was aware of a complete covering of angels' wings over the whole room. She described this to the others present and they all took it as a sign that Gerald Pimentel was the right minister for their church to appoint.

In the Old Testament it was sometimes necessary for God to act decisively on behalf of His people, the

Israelites. Sennacherib, the King of Assyria, was attacking the cities of Judah and threatening to capture Jerusalem. He openly ridiculed and blasphemed against God, considering Him no more powerful than the "gods" of the other nations he had destroyed. King Hezekiah in Jerusalem brought the matter to the Lord God in prayer. Through Isaiah the prophet, God replied to King Hezekiah that because Sennacherib had "insulted and blasphemed ... he will not enter the city; I, the Lord, will defend and save it." The account continues, "That night the angel of the Lord went out and put to death a hundred and eighty-five thousand of the men in the Assyrian camp. When the people got up the next morning there were all the dead bodies. So Sennacherib, King of Assyria, broke camp and withdrew." He returned to the temple of the god he worshiped and was killed there by his own sons (2 Kings 19:35-6).

At the end of the Bible, Revelation reveals that this "angel of judgment" will carry out God's plan for the end of the world, when Jesus will return. At that time, God's angels will fulfil His will in judging those who deliberately reject Jesus and the salvation He has provided. We are all sinners, and if forgiveness of sins is not received, the penalty for sins, which is death, will have to be paid at Judgment Day (Matthew 13:49-50). We are also told in Revelation that, in his vision of heaven, John saw "many angels, numbering ten thousand times ten thousand"—that's a hundred million! This shows us evocatively how God is so much more worthy of our praise than we generally realize or consider.

# CHAPTER SEVEN

# *Unseen Angels*

uch beautiful singing," "thousands of voices blending together," "descants so high and harmonies so complex," "an amazing ethereal quality": these are some of the descriptions given by people who believe they have heard angels. One even said: "If this is what heaven is like, I can't wait to get there!"

All those who have been privileged to hear such music report that the singing was heavenly, beautiful and evocative. All, without exception, sensed that it was miraculous to hear it. In this kind of angel experience there is nothing to see, but hearing thousands of such voices can obviously be overwhelming.

Often, the angelic singing has been heard by more than one person at a time. Audrey Nicholls, for example, was with three others. While on a day trip to Scarborough in 1957, Audrey's widowed father unexpectedly collapsed and died. Knowing that Audrey would be devastated by his death, her aunt Alice and uncle Arthur, with their eighteen-year-old son, Keith, came to stay with her as soon as they heard the news.

"They even," she recalls, "brought the Sunday joint with them in their haste to be by my side."

The evening before the funeral, they were all together in the kitchen, when suddenly they were "rooted to the spot by the most beautiful singing." "I am sure," says Audrey, "that if I had been on my own and had related what happened, people would have said I was imagining things because I was in a state of shock. But I believe the Lord permitted it to happen to four of us at once so that people could not deny its validity."

No one moved or spoke for several minutes until Audrey asked her uncle, who was nearest the door, to go and see what it was. He undid the lock, and, as he opened the door, the singing ceased. They felt privileged to have had this wonderful experience.

One of the recurrent features of people hearing angelic choirs is that it is unmistakably different from the sound of human voices. The experience of Les and Mary Newall, who live in Bolton, is typical of many. They were visiting Tewkesbury one summer, and had gone out for an evening stroll after dinner. Finding an old church, they wandered in for a look around. Everything was quiet and not a soul was about. "By the side of the church," they write, "was a beautiful walled garden, and we spent some time looking at it through the iron gate. It was so peaceful, not even the sound of traffic. Suddenly there was a great swelling of *the* most beautiful music, like a huge choir singing a tremendous harmonic sound. We looked at each other in amazement."

Afterward, they often talked and puzzled over what had happened but it was not until some years later that they became committed Christians and understood where the singing had come from. Later, in

Yorkshire, they witnessed something that answered the puzzle for them about the angelic choir they heard that evening in Tewkesbury. Not only Les and Mary Newall, but also two other families have written to tell me about an amazing event which was heard by a great many people at the Yorkshire Showground. Thousands of Christians had gathered there in 1983 for Dales Bible Week, a camp for teaching, worship and relaxation. On three different nights, at about midnight, the police received complaints from local residents living nearby, about the "loud swells of singing" coming from the showground. Each time the police arrived to sort out "the over-enthusiastic worshippers" they found the whole camp absolutely silent and the pavilion, where the meetings were held and where the sound had come from, deserted and in darkness. Other local residents, however, enjoyed the "most beautiful music" and called at the gates during the day to inquire who had been singing so exquisitely. The Christian campers heard the wondrous choir as well. As Les says, "Humans weren't singing but the angels were, and the sound we heard could not have been made by human voices, however good they were."

Occasionally an angelic choir is heard by some but not all the people present. Olive O'Brien and her sister, Margaret Gregory, are the daughters of a builder and his lapsed Catholic wife. In the winter of 1950, their father was known to be dying, and the family had gathered around his bedside. About 3 A.M. Olive heard heavenly singing coming from outside the window. She did not say anything, but after listening for a few minutes, Margaret said, "Can you hear singing?" Olive was delighted that someone else could hear it too. The strange thing was that another sister and their mother, who was slightly deaf, did not hear anything. It seems it was just for Olive and Margaret.

Frances Whitby was engaged in a very ordinary activity—cleaning the bathroom—when she suddenly heard the most beautiful music and singing. A friend staying with them was outside, washing his car, and Frances thought that if his car music was sounding that loud indoors, it would soon bother the neighbors. She went outside, and found he was not playing music at all. She asked others in the house if they had heard music, but nobody had. She went back to the bathroom and did not hear it again, but felt the Lord telling her that all the time the angels are praising Him and giving Him glory in heaven.

During the mid 1960s Joan Earle and her mother were staying in Cornwall. While there, they visited the tiny hermit chapel on Rame Head. As they approached it, walking down the grassy headland, they were surprised to hear singing coming from the building. They listened for a while and then two people came out. Joan says, "We asked them about the singing and if a service was being held, but they told us no one was inside! Afterward we called on the local rector of Kingsand and Cawsand, to tell him of our experience. He was not at all surprised, as on other occasions people had reported hearing singing. This convinced us that we had indeed heard angels and for us it will always remain a wonderful and unique experience."

Many people, including my family and myself, have heard the magnificence of angelic singing on cassette tape! Four members of a worship group at a church in Surrey were practising a chorus "Alleluia, Alleluia" in an otherwise empty church. They recorded what their little group had sung with guitar accompaniment but, when they played back the tape, they were staggered to hear hundreds of voices singing. To all who hear this, it is a wondrous sound, which makes us glorify God. The descants are much higher than human voices can reach and the harmonies are so intricate; it makes truly thrilling listening.

Sometimes a voice gives a message: it may be information or an instruction about something requiring action. Such was the case one night in 1963 when Margaret Peart and her husband, Albert, had gone to bed. Albert was already asleep, and Margaret was dozing when, she reports, "I sensed a strong, overpowering presence in the room, which seemed to be ten feet tall and I heard a voice say, 'Don't be afraid. You must pray for Mr. Robson.' Mr. Robson was someone we both knew. I had worked for him and he had been a great support to me after my father died. A few days earlier I had heard he was seriously ill following a heart attack and was not expected to survive. I was too embarrassed to wake Albert, as we had not been married long and had never talked about God or prayer. So, in my mind I said, 'Yes, I'll pray for Mr. Robson,' but the reply came, 'You and Albert must pray.' I still had the audacity to argue, 'No, I won't wake Albert up. What will he think of me? He may become annoyed.' The presence insisted that Albert be involved and, to my astonishment, I felt my mouth being opened for me and heard my voice say, 'Albert, wake up. Can we say a prayer for Mr. Robson?'"

"Albert woke immediately and didn't ask any questions. He simply prayed with me, turned over and went back to sleep. The presence left, leaving me feeling confused. My mind tried to make sense of the experience. I realized I had not opened my eyes to see this presence, but I hadn't needed to. It felt more real than Albert who was lying beside me. Even though it was so powerful, there was an inner assurance that I had nothing to fear. Albert's response also surprised me. He joined in as if he had been prepared. Mr. Robson did recover and maybe God had commissioned the angel to find someone who cared for him dearly to pray for his healing that night."

Christine Zwart had been every week to visit her friend, Laura, who was seriously ill in the hospital, until she went on a vacation to Yorkshire with her family, when she was unable to visit Laura. One night she woke up and heard a voice she did not recognize. The voice was not in her head but external, clear and definite, saying, "Do you realize Laura has just died?" She went back to sleep and in the morning when the phone rang, she said to her husband, "That will be Tim [Laura's husband] because Laura has died." It was, indeed, Tim with that message, and Christine is sure that it was an angel who had spoken to her during the night.

The following three reports of unseen angels using a voice, when nobody is visible, all happened in South Dorset. Mrs. Elizabeth Rose, of Bournemouth had suffered terrible pains for eighteen years after an operation in 1970 for cancer. The pains occurred two or three times a week, and would last anything from six to twenty-four hours. She kept asking the doctors for relief from the pain, saying that it was worse than childbirth. "At least all the childbirth pain has a worthwhile result!" she said ruefully. However nothing could be done medically to help her. One day, standing in the kitchen, she heard a voice say clearly, "You will not have any more pains." As Mrs. Rose says, "This seemed too good to be true! But it *is* true!" This happened over two years before she told me about it and she had not suffered any pain since.

Peter Davies, who lived in Poole at the time he heard an angelic voice, was concerned that a haulage job he had been asked to do by his supervisor was neither legal nor safe. He refused to do it, but was told, "You will do it tomorrow, or you are out of work." This dilemma bothered him, so that evening he went to talk it over with a friend. They decided Peter should go to visit his boss, so he set off alone to drive to the man's house. Peter is quite certain that on the way he heard a voice from the back seat of the car say crisply: "Don't go round." It was so real, that he looked over his shoulder to see who spoke, but, as he knew, he was alone. He changed directions and went home. The next day, Peter discovered that the supervisor had dealt with the matter himself. The voice had saved him from a show-down with his boss and his problem had been solved without intervention from Peter himself.

Jill Deverill heard a similar voice when she worked as a supervisor for the residential wardens of housing complexes for the elderly. This involved considerable travel alone across southern England. One morning, as she was about to get into her car, she heard a voice tell her to check the rear offside tire. She ignored it and opened the car door, but the voice repeated the message more insistently. This time, she went to look and found that tire in need of air. She drove carefully to a garage, and dealt with the tire, but was told by the garage attendant that, on the motorway, with a tire in that state, she would certainly have lost control of the car.

Hearing voices cannot always be the sign of an angel speaking. People who frequently hear voices in-

side their heads may be unwell. But the three
incidents described above were notably once-in-a-
lifetime experiences which came unexpectedly to
committed Christians. These were not people who
suffered from any form of mental illness, nor were
they expecting any supernatural intervention. Each of
them has had just this one experience of hearing a
clear voice without seeing the speaker.

A note of caution needs to be sounded here, because the Bible teaches that Satan can also speak
with an audible voice. It is widely accepted that seeking after visions or unusual experiences can open up
someone to evil influence. With a vision or a sup-
posed appearance of an angel, the test appears to be
whether peace is tangibly felt. If something heard or
seen is not in line with the Bible's teaching, and does
not give a sense of peace, then it is probably not of
God.

A nun, Sister Mary Clare, also heard a voice giving her a message. In 1967 she was reading for a
science degree at Newcastle University and was becoming anxious with all the study. She took a book
on yoga out of the library and went to her room to try
some of the meditation exercises. Suddenly a masculine voice spoke quite distinctly with a firm tone,
"Don't mess about with that, it's dangerous." This
gave her such a shock that she did not even open the
book, but took it straight back to the library. The
warning prevented her from entering into experiences
which would not have been helpful.

Other reports tell of unseen hands giving protection from danger. In December 1990, at Brent Cross
shopping center, London, an elderly Dorset lady
called Rene Pease was going down an escalator with
her daughter-in-law. Unfortunately, as she stepped on

to the escalator, she tripped and landed on one knee. Normally her knees are too stiff and painful to enable her to raise herself to a standing position and, while traveling down the escalator, she found it impossible to get up. Her daughter-in-law, laden with shopping, was not near enough to help her, so all she could do was call out, "Get up, Mum, or it will be dreadful when you get to the bottom." Seized with near panic, Rene suddenly felt amazingly calm and, although no one was near enough to help, she felt hands behind and beside her gently lift her up. Her daughter-in-law had also felt surprisingly calm, and both of them knew it was an angel who had come to the rescue.

Another incident occurred a few years ago to Monica Dyer, who was painting her bungalow in Shanklin, on the Isle of Wight. "I was perched," she reports, "at the top of a ladder when I overreached myself, the ladder slid sideways and I found myself falling toward some stone steps." She had been suffering from spinal trouble so, fearing a serious injury, she prayed to God to help her. Monica continues, "I distinctly felt feathered wings on either side of my body, gently laying me down against the top step. When I ventured to move, I was astounded to find I had no pain or bruises whatsoever!"

Wyn Owston is a retired doctor who lives in Chorleywood, Hertfordshire. Forty years ago, Wyn sat her six-month-old daughter, Rosie, down in the kitchen, happily munching a rusk. She went out to the scullery and was horrified to find her washing machine had detached itself from its moorings while in the spin cycle and was careering toward her. With difficulty, she managed to get around to unplug it and was relieved when it stopped moving. Just then, she felt someone touch her left shoulder and looked

around, but no one was there. She immediately
thought of Rosie and dashed back into the kitchen to
find her blue from choking on the rusk. She picked
up Rosie and held her upside down by her ankles and
was able to hook out the piece of rusk from her throat
so she could breathe again. Wyn writes, "Who had
touched my shoulder? I am convinced it was an angel." Rosie survived the event and is now a doctor
herself.

Roy Scott, who lives in Oxfordshire, had always
dreaded the thought of being with a dying person,
perhaps because it was not something he had ever encountered before. His wife, Hilary, had been in and
out of the local hospice for pain relief in her struggle
against cancer. On March 10, 1992, Hilary was in the
hospice, but there had been no expectation that the
end was near. Roy came to visit her and sat beside
her bed from 2 P.M. During this time they both experienced healing which was not physical, but at a
much deeper level. This meant that Hilary, although
knowing that she was dying of cancer, came to death
with a great sense of assurance and faith, from the
knowledge that she had been healed in her soul. Roy
says, "It felt like a very holy thing, as though we
were surrounded by angels." Hilary died at 7 P.M. and
it was so peaceful in the room that Roy stayed there,
with family members joining him, for several hours.
He experienced none of the terror he had anticipated
feeling at such a time. He sensed that the whole room
was full of angels and he realized that it was "holy."

Following this experience, two or three months
later Roy was able to visit a friend who was very ill.
He said to her, "It's amazingly peaceful here," and
she felt the same. On a later visit, when his friend
was dying, Roy again felt the extraordinary sense of

peace, stillness and holiness that he had felt at Hil-
ry's death. It felt like a comfortably familiar situation.
Roy had never had an experience like this before Hilary died, and would never have thought it possible
that he could have felt "comfortable" at such a time.

A further example of God's protection came when
Roger Boulter, a middle-aged man from Birmingham,
walked past some threatening drunken youths. One of
them, who stood only about a foot away, was particularly angry and abusive, so Roger prayed desperately for the Lord to protect him. He says, "From the
moment I prayed, I felt strongly that there was an angel in the small space between the youth and me.
Nothing vague, but a definite presence occupying a
physical space, about the same size as a tall human
being. The young man tried to hit me a few times,
but didn't seem able to get his fist across to me. He
was obviously near enough, but eventually gave up,
swore and walked off." Roger was sure this unseen
angel had saved him from a nasty attack.

None of these reports include evidence of anything
visible. But the effect they had on the people concerned is clear enough: in every case, the individuals
were thoroughly convinced they had received angelic
assistance.

## CHAPTER EIGHT

# *Angels in History*

he majority of the accounts in this book concern the experiences of contemporary people, who have seen and heard angels during their own lifetime. These I have set in the context of the Biblical accounts of angelic appearances, to show that the same angels were in operation then as now. This chapter traces a few of the incidents that have occurred during the two thousand years in between, all of which bear a similar ring of authenticity.

The earliest account I have found, in *Angels* by a "Bible Student," is of St. Cecilia, who lived in Rome in the second to third century AD, when Christians were being persecuted and martyred by the Romans. She lived a pure and holy life, dedicating her soul and body to God. But, against her will, her parents gave her in marriage to a Roman named Valerian. On their wedding night, Cecilia told him, "Valerian, I have a secret to tell you. There is a beautiful angel who guards me and he will permit no one to harm me." Valerian replied, "Show me this angel and I will be a Christian too." Cecilia said, "If you believe in the one living and true God and are baptized, you will see the angel." Valerian readily agreed, so Cecilia told him to go and find an elderly blind man out on the road, who would lead him to where the Bishop was in hiding, to escape the persecution.

When Valerian returned after being baptized, he saw Cecilia praying on her knees, and beside her stood an angel, whose divine light filled the whole room. He was so awestruck that he fetched his brother, Tibertius, who also heard the truth of Jesus Christ from Cecilia and was sent out to be baptized. On returning, Tibertius, too, saw the angel and the glorious divine light. By now the two young men were so full of God's Holy Spirit that they went out and preached openly about Christ. Sadly, they were arrested and martyred for their faith. The judge, Almachius, who had sentenced them to death, hearing that they were rich, wished to have their wealth for himself. Learning that one had been married to Cecilia, he sent for her demanding the men's possessions, but was incensed to learn that they had already been distributed among the poor. Furious, he ordered a furnace to be lighted and Cecilia to be thrown into it. However an angel was seen to be walking with Cecilia in the fire and she was unharmed.

This is similar to the account of the three men in the book of Daniel who were tied up and thrown by a vengeful king into a "burning, fiery furnace." Those outside also saw a fourth man, an angel, and all four walked around in the fire, unbound and unharmed. Eventually they were allowed out and not even their hair or clothes were scorched, although the heat of the fire had killed the soldiers who threw them in (Daniel 3:13–30). In exactly the same way,

for a day and a night, Cecilia remained in the fire,
but not a hair of her head, nor even her clothing was
touched by the flames. Almachius then ordered that
Cecilia be beheaded, but, even then, it took the exe-
cutioner three unsuccessful attempts to behead her
and it was a further three days until she died.

As happened in the Bible to Abraham and Sarah
(Genesis 18) and to Manoah's wife (Judges 13), there
are several accounts of women being visited by an
angel to tell them that the child they were expecting
would be specially holy. This happened to the mother
of St. Fintan of Cloneenagh, in the early seventh century. The boy possessed the gifts of prophecy and
knowledge, and became a monk and later an abbot. It
is reported that St. Columba of Iona saw a vision of
the abbot Fintan standing among the angels before
the judgment seat of Christ every Sunday night. Columba sent a disciple to seek out this abbot in Ireland
to make his acquaintance and learn from him. Columba described him as a man "saint-like and come-
ly, with a ruddy face and gleaming eyes."

Monica was born in 332 AD in North Africa. She
was patient and gentle; her prayers and example re-
sulted in her violent husband and cantankerous
mother-in-law, who lived with them, becoming Christians. In later years her prayers focused on her brilliant son Augustine who was wasting his brains and
his opportunities in living a wayward life. She was
encouraged by seeing a radiant angel in a vision. She
seemed to be standing on a wooden beam, be-
moaning her son's downfall, when the angel appeared
and asked her to dry her eyes. "Your son is with
you," the angel said and she saw Augustine standing
on the beam beside her. This was prophetic, because
it was another nine years before Augustine was con-

verted. He went on to be ordained a priest and later
to become Bishop of Hippo, in North Africa, for
thirty-five years. He wrote extensively, the best
known of his writings being the *Confessions,* contain-
ing his famous phrase:

> *You made us for Yourself*
> *and our hearts find no peace*
> *until they rest in You.*

St. Francis of Assisi was born in Italy in about
1182. He was from a wealthy family and initially
spent his inheritance lavishly. In his early twenties he
went to join some fighting in southern Italy when he
was taken ill at Spoleto. During his illness, he heard
a heavenly voice tell him to return home and "serve
the Master rather than the man." We do not know if
he saw an angel, or just heard the voice. However,
this was a turning point for Francis who, from that
moment on, devotedly served his master, Jesus
Christ.

Joan of Arc lived only nineteen years (1412–31)
but she became the national heroine of France. An il-
literate, though devout peasant girl from Domrémy, at
the age of thirteen she began to hear a voice accompanied by "a great light." As time went on, she realized that it was the archangel Michael speaking to
her, giving her specific instructions. Later she was
able to see him too and she also heard the voices of
two others, whom she identified as St. Catherine and
St. Margaret. Being interrogated later, as to the validity of her visions, Joan said the archangel Michael
had appeared before her eyes and he was not alone,
but was accompanied by the angels of heaven. Asked
if she saw the angels physically, Joan replied, "I saw

them with my physical eye, as well as I see you."
The question was a trap, since at that time angels
were thought not to be able to appear bodily, but Joan
did not know that; she merely told what she saw. She
added, "When they left me, I wept; and I heartily
wished they had taken me away with them." She was
repeatedly asked questions about the visions and
eventually she replied only, "Believe me or not, as
you like."

The purpose of Joan's visions was to encourage the
French army in their fight against the invading English who sought to take the French throne. The
French officers, dismayed by the advances of the ag-
gressors, could not believe that this slip of a girl who
presented herself at the court could change the for-
tunes of the defeated army. Questioned as to her reason for demanding an audience with Charles, the
dauphin (the heir to the throne), she replied that she
could not read or write, but she knew voices had
commanded her to raise the siege of Orléans and
crown the king at Rheims. The courtiers decided to
test Joan by taking her into the presence of the dauphin whom she had previously never met or seen.
Charles was disguised as an ordinary courtier and
someone else was wearing his majestic clothes. But
Joan was not deceived, and immediately went to
Charles saying, "I am God's messenger to tell you
that you are to be the true king of France."

While following the angel's directions Joan had
unparalleled success in inspiring the French army to
victory. Still only seventeen, she led the victorious
soldiers to Rheims where Charles was crowned in
great splendor. At the coronation, Joan saw an angel
bring a crown to the king and "over three hundred
people present had seen it too." Her mission com-

pleted, Joan wanted to go back to the simple village life she missed, but she was never allowed to return. Sadly her victories on the battlefield, which made her the heroine of the common people, caused jealousy of her at the royal court. In 1430 Joan was captured by the Duke of Burgundy who was fighting on the English side. The cowardly French king, Charles, did nothing to save the girl who had helped him so much. After a long and unfair trial, she was condemned as a witch because of the voices she had heard. She was burnt in the marketplace at Rouen; a sad end for the girl who sought no honor for herself, but had been used by God to rescue France from English rule.

Teresa of Avila (1515-82) was a Carmelite nun who experienced visions and visits by angels which a priest judged to be from God. One day, according to Butler's *Lives of the Saints,* Teresa, while reciting "Veni Creator Spiritus," heard these words spoken to her: "I will not have you hold conversation with men, but with angels." From then on, she heard speeches "even more distinct and clear than those which men hear with their bodily ears." These filled her with an assurance of truth, joy and peace which is seen in her famous writings, especially the *Way of Perfection.*

John Milton (1608–74) wrote much about angels in his works *Paradise Lost* and *Paradise Regained.* He also included angels in some of his shorter poems, such as "Ode on the Morning of Christ's Nativity" and "Blest Pair of Sirens," but there is no evidence to suggest that he saw angels himself. Many other poets have written fictional works about angels, including Dante, John Henry Newman and Henry Longfellow. Only William Blake (1757–1827), however, the English poet and artist, said he saw visions of angels frequently from his childhood into adulthood. He painted and wrote about them and, during the last few years of his life, illustrated many of the visions he had seen. Sometimes, as he was painting, he would suddenly stop and remark matter-of-factly, "I can't go on—it is gone!" William Blake was a man of great natural, if somewhat undisciplined, genius. A truly loving soul, he was neglected and misunderstood by most of his contemporaries, but he led a cheerful and contented life, illuminated by vision. Referring to angels, Blake once said, "The way people feel now, and the ruling ideas of the modern age, have made the angels weak." He tried, by his art and poetry, to counteract that.

In 1859 the Welsh Revival affected thousands of people and changed many lives. There were clear indications of increasing spiritual activity and, within twelve months, every county in Wales had felt its effects. Eifon Evans, in his book, *When He is Come,* reported that "An unusual phenomenon in this revival was the 'singing in the air' which many reliable witnesses had heard. The sound of heavenly angelic voices, sweetly and softly joined in harmony, without any apparent melody, was overpowering. The effect on the hearer was to render him as incapable of movement as though nailed to the spot." The later Welsh Revival of 1904–5 also had many occasions of angelic singing being heard, when God's Holy Spirit was coming mightily upon the people and changing many lives.

A remarkable man, Sadhu Sundar Singh, was born in India on September 3, 1889. His father was a wealthy landowner, who gave Sundar every opportunity to receive a good education and achieve a high position in society. His mother was a refined and gifted lady who taught her brilliant son to search for peace through his learning. During his childhood he studied unceasingly the holy writings of the Sikhs, the Hindus and the Moslems, but nowhere could he find the peace he sought. One of the highlights of his young life was being taken by his mother to visit an elderly holy man, a *sadhu,* who lived alone in the jungle. Sundar was sent by his father to the best school in the area, which was run by Christian missionaries, but he hated Christians and the Bible, making life very difficult for the teachers and his friends who had become Christians. His mother died when he was fourteen and then his search became even more ardent for *shanti,* which in Hindi means "peace, full satisfaction of the soul."

The following year Sundar prayed one night that, if there was a God, He would reveal Himself to him. He was so desperate to know true peace that, if his prayers went unanswered, Sundar had decided to commit suicide by throwing himself in front of an express train that went past his home at 5 A.M. He woke at 3 A.M., took his early morning bath, which Hindus and Sikhs always have before worship, and returned to his room to pray. He lifted his head, opened his eyes and was surprised to see a cloud of light in the room, while everything else was in darkness. The light got brighter and then he saw the radiant figure of Jesus Christ, who asked, "Why do you persecute Me? I died on the cross for you and the whole world." As Jesus spoke, Sundar fell prostrate and worshiped Him. When the cloud disappeared he went to wake his father to tell of this experience which led him to become a Christian.

Sundar's family tried to make him change his mind, poisoned him and banished him from the home and his inheritance, so at fifteen he began a wander-

ing life, learning more about Jesus wherever he could
and speaking about Jesus to anyone who would listen. He became respected as a Christian *sadhu*. He
had three angel experiences of which I have read.
Once, Sundar was feeling rather low as he walked
along from one village to another. Another man
joined him and talked so encouragingly that Sundar
was feeling much better by the time they reached the
next village. Just then he found he was alone, the
other man having vanished. He was certain the Lord
had sent an angel to encourage him. On another occasion he was walking in the Himalayas along a forest path, which came to a river too wide to cross. It
was near nightfall and it was a dangerous place to be
alone at night, with wild animals about. He looked up
and saw a man warming himself by a fire; the man
called out, "Don't worry, I am coming to help you."
He stepped into the river and came across to Sundar.
Putting him on his shoulders he carried Sundar
across, but when Sundar got down on the other side
there was no trace of either the man or the fire.

The third time Sundar received angelic help was
when he was arrested in a town called Rasa, in Tibet.
He was taken before the head lama and accused of
teaching Christianity, a "foreign" religion. His sentence was to be thrown into a dry well where many
people had previously been left to die. The top was
covered with a locked lid and Sundar was trapped
among the decaying flesh and bones to rot away in
complete darkness. He thought, "My God, why have
You forsaken me?" Some hours later, he heard the lid
being removed and saw a rope descending. A voice
said, "Take hold of the rope." Making a loop to support himself under his arms Sundar was pulled up
and enjoyed breathing fresh air again. There was no

sign at all of his rescuer, but he was delighted to be free. The following day he was again publicly teaching about Jesus. When the head lama heard about it, he had Sundar arrested again, and angrily demanded to know how he had escaped. There was only one key for the lock of the lid, so the lama assumed it had been stolen. He was amazed to find the key still attached to his own belt. He immediately dismissed Sundar telling him to leave the area, but not daring to punish him any further.

Here in the West, Christian churches and cathedrals have been elaborately decorated with paintings, sometimes whole walls and ceilings, like the Sistine Chapel in Rome. Wood carvings, stained glass windows, embroidery, stone and marble statues are all ways of portraying Christian teaching through art. It can be difficult to translate what can be vividly expressed verbally into a dynamic and lifelike form pictorially. With angels in particular, realistically portraying "extraordinarily brilliant," "dazzling," "shining with great intensity" is quite a challenge. Some artists have managed to achieve evocative colored pictures of angels, but it is certainly more difficult to show brilliance in a pen and ink drawing, especially the eyes of the angel which are particularly dynamic.

Within their own tradition, the artists of East and West have depicted angels according to the understanding and vision of each period. The Byzantine Empire (fourth to fourteenth centuries) produced art which is primarily concerned with teaching truth and set a standard for Christian art. Today, the art of the Eastern Orthodox Church still follows the tradition of Byzantine art. Orthodox paintings of angels seek to convey strength, heavenly power, serenity and speed of flight. If the Byzantine angels do not move us by

their beauty, they should inspire us with their strength
and give us confidence. One should always feel safe
in their presence.

In the thirteenth century angels were usually portrayed with powerful wings, flowing white robes and
bare feet. Sometimes they held scrolls or musical instruments and were strikingly masculine in appearance. In the first half of the sixteenth century, many
statues in churches were mutilated because they were
considered idolatrous. Thankfully there are many
which were not damaged, including impressive sur-
viving ones in Lincoln Cathedral and Westminster
Abbey.

The Renaissance was a period of rebirth in the arts
and learning in Italy and on into other parts of Eu-
rope during the fourteenth to sixteenth centuries.
New ideas and art techniques brought about a great
surge in the quantity and quality of art. The study of
perspective and the anatomy of the human body
meant artists could give dimension to their scenes,
moving away from the lifeless figures on flat back-
grounds of earlier times. Sweeping over walls and
ceilings, angels appeared more like humans with
wings. Often they were given elaborate clothing and
footwear, sometimes brightly colored. People today
have sometimes described the garments of angels as
colorful, but generally in pastel shades.

The ability of flight in angels seemed to capture
artists' imaginations, enabling whole canvases to be
filled with activity, having people in the lower half
and angels above. The angels portrayed in nine-
teenth-century art are much less ornate. Protestantism
had called for more simplicity, so angels tended to be
unelaborate, even insipid, wearing simple gowns,
usually white. This is where the idea of feminine an-

gels seems to have come from, although most people in telling me of angels they have seen speak of them as strong and masculine in appearance. In Victorian times angels became sentimentalized and overly human-looking. From the Renaissance period until the present, the portrayal of angels has become gradually more and more human, rather than heavenly. Perhaps this coincides with man's eyes focusing more on earthly and scientific matters and less on the spiritual truth of God.

Many churches around Great Britain have pictures or statues of angels, particularly the churches called St. Michael and All Angels. Perhaps one of the most dynamic bronze statues of recent years is the only one by Sir Jacob Epstein on the outer wall of the entrance to Coventry Cathedral. He worked it during his seventies between 1955 and 1958. St. Michael is depicted as a powerful winged figure, over twelve feet tall, with his foot holding down the Devil in submission. It is a dramatic portrayal, which does true justice to the cathedral. Considering how many angels are seen in art, in the works of old masters, and statues in churches around England, it is surprising how little consideration we give to them.

## CHAPTER NINE

# *Angels in World War I*

wo remarkable events occurred during World War I that afterward were referred to by the troops as "The Angels of Mons" and "The White Cavalry." At the time, controversy raged as to whether the reports were true or false. Were they just the imaginings of battle-weary men, or fiction created by journalists?

The first of these events occurred near the town of Mons during a battle between the German and Allied armies on August 23 and 24, 1914. After sweeping aside all resistance, the German army had advanced on a wide front, right into the heart of Belgium and France. Although the Belgians, French and British put up a stout defense, it was principally against the British that the heaviest enemy attacks were being launched. British troops were greatly outnumbered, and had had no respite for days, losing many men and guns in the severe fighting. Serious defeat looked inevitable, especially as practically no reserve forces were available. Back home, churches had been crowded with the British people who had been called to a National Day of Prayer for the future of the Allied forces looked bleak. A number of remarkable incidents occurred in the following weeks, which held back the German forces long enough to allow the British army to withdraw to comparative safety.

*The Times* correspondent prematurely telegraphed unnecessarily alarming news that the British army had been "annihilated at Mons," ending with the words, "We must set our teeth and bear it." However, next day news came that a disaster had been averted by a miraculous turn of events.

The following account, taken from *The Angels of Mons* published by E. Austin & Son in 1916, was written by two British officers:

*The British expected annihilation, as we were almost helpless, when to our amazement the Germans stood like dazed men, never so much as touched their guns, nor stirred till we had turned round and escaped by some crossroads. One man said he saw "a troop of angels" between us and the enemy. He has been a changed man ever since. Another man was asked if he had heard the wonderful stories of angels. He said he had SEEN them himself. When he and his company were retreating, they heard the German cavalry tearing after them. They saw a place where they thought a stand might be made, with sure hope of safety; but, before they could reach it, the German cavalry were upon them. They therefore turned round and faced the enemy, expecting nothing but instant death,*

*when to their wonder, they saw, between them
and the enemy, a whole troop of angels. The
German horses turned round terrified and regularly stampeded. The men tugged at their bri-
dles, while the poor beasts tore away in every
direction from our men.*

Captain Cecil Wightwick Hayward, Staff Officer in
the 1st Corps Intelligence, British Army Headquarters,
gave testimony to what he knew. The following was
printed in *This England* in the winter 1982 edition.

*While a detachment of British soldiers was re-
tiring through Mons under very heavy gun-fire,
they knelt behind a hastily erected barricade
and endeavored to hold up the enemy advance.
The firing on both sides was very intensive and
the air reverberated with deafening crashes of
exploding shells. Suddenly, firing on both sides
stopped dead and a silence fell. Looking over
their barrier, the astonished British saw four or
five wonderful beings much bigger than men between themselves and the Germans. They were
white-robed and bare-headed, and seemed
rather to float than stand. Their backs were toward the British, and they faced the Germans
with out-stretched arms and hands. The sun was
shining quite brightly at the time. Next thing the
British knew was that the Germans were retreating in great disorder.*

The account of Captain Hayward continues:

*On another occasion, the British were in danger
of being surrounded by the Germans, and had*

*lost numbers of guns and men. Just when mat-*
*ters seemed hopeless, the heavy enemy fire sud-*
*denly stopped dead and a great silence fell over*
*all. The sky opened with a bright shining light*
*and figures of "luminous beings" appeared.*
*They seemed to float between the British and*
*the German forces, and to prevent the further*
*advance of the enemy. Some of the German cav-*
*alry were advancing and the officers and men*
*were unable to get their horses to go forward.*
*Before the surprised British were able to realize*
*what had happened, the whole of the apparently*
*victorious enemy force were retreating in great*
*disorder. This allowed the British and Allied ar-*
*mies to re-form and fall back upon a line of de-*
*fense several miles further west.*

Many German prisoners were taken that day who
surrendered when there was no need to do so. Some
were asked afterward why they had, "for there were
many more of you than of us; we were a mere hand-
ful." The Germans looked amazed and replied, "But
there were hosts and hosts of you." It was thought
that the angels appeared to them as reinforcements
of the Allied ranks.

The official German version was given in a letter
to the editor of the *Church Times* printed on July 28,
1915.

*We simply could not go on . . . we were power-*
*less. A German lieutenant when asked why the*
*men had failed to continue their charge, for*
*which they had been severely blamed at Berlin,*
*replied: "I cannot tell you. I only know that we*

*were charging full on the British and in a mo-*
*ment we were stopped ... there was nothing at*
*all, only our horses swerved round and fled and*
*we could do nothing!*

An animal reacted in a similar way in a Biblical
account. In Numbers 22, Balaam was pressing his
donkey to go forward and he stubbornly refused because he saw an angel on the path. Balaam only discovered that this was the reason for the donkey's
refusal when he, too, saw the angel.

William Foggitt of Thirsk, North Yorkshire, re-
called his father returning from the Sunday evening
service at Thirsk Methodist Chapel some time in
1919. He reported that he had heard "a wonderful
sermon from a young man who had fought at the battle of Mons in August 1914." The soldier had said
that he had come across a wounded German solider
who was pointing excitedly to the sky. "I bent down
to give him a drink from my water bottle and the
German soldier gasped, 'Angels, angels, they hef
stopped us.' "

As the forces were retreating from Mons over the
next few days there were further sightings. A letter
printed in the *Evening News* on September 14 from a
distinguished lieutenant-colonel stated:

*On the night of the 27th, I was riding along in*
*the column with two other officers. We had been*
*talking and doing our best to keep from falling*
*asleep on our horses. As we rode along I be-*
*came conscious of the fact that, in the fields on*
*both sides of the road along which we were*
*marching, I could see a very large body of*
*horsemen. These horsemen had the appearance*

*of squadrons of cavalry, and they seemed to be riding across the fields and going in the same direction as we were going and keeping level with us. The night was not very dark, and I fancied that I could see squadron upon squadron of these cavalry men quite distinctly. I did not say a word about it at first, but I watched them for about twenty minutes.*

*The other two officers had stopped talking. At last one of them asked me if I saw anything in the fields. I then told him what I had seen. The third officer then confessed that he, too, had been watching these horsemen for the past twenty minutes. So convinced were we that they were really cavalry that, at the next halt, one of the officers took a party of men out to reconnoitre, and found no one there. The night then grew darker and we saw no more. The same phenomenon was seen by many men in our column. Of course, we were all dog-tired and over-taxed, but it is an extraordinary thing that the same phenomenon should be witnessed by so many different people. I myself am absolutely convinced that I saw those horsemen; and I feel sure that they did not exist only in my imagination. I do not attempt to explain the mystery—I only state facts.*

It is obvious from the tone of his account that the lieutenant-colonel considered these horsemen to be protective rather than hostile.

The *Evening News* reported a further account, which was confirmed as accurate, relating to the following day:

*I was with my battalion in the retreat from
Mons on or about August 28th. The German
cavalry were expected to make a charge, and
we were waiting to fire. The weather was very
hot and clear, and between eight and nine
o'clock in the evening I was standing with a
party of nine other men on duty, and some distance on either side there were parties of ten on
guard. An officer suddenly came up to us in a
state of great anxiety and asked us if we had
seen anything astonishing. Taking me and some
others a few yards away he showed us the sky.
I could see quite plainly in mid-air a strange
light which seemed to be quite distinctly out-
lined and was not a reflection of the moon, nor
were there any clouds in the neighborhood. The
light became brighter and I could see quite distinctly three shapes, one in the center having
what looked like outspread wings; the other two
were not so large, but were quite plainly distinct
from the center one. They appeared to have a
long loose-hanging garment of a golden tint,
and they were above the German line facing us.
We stood watching them for about three-
quarters of an hour. All the men with me saw
them, and other men came up from other groups
who told us that they had seen the same thing.
I have not the slightest doubt that we saw what
I now tell you. I shall never forget it as long
as I live. I lie awake in bed and picture it all as
I saw it that night. Of my battalion there are
now only five men alive besides myself, and I
have no hope of ever getting back to the front.
I have a record of fifteen years' good service,*

*and I should be very sorry to make a fool of myself by telling a story merely to please anyone.*

Those who found it hard to believe that God could intervene so decisively to help the forces trying to prevent the German army from capturing smaller nations looked for an alternative explanation. On September 29, the *Evening News* published a story entitled "The Bowmen" by a celebrated author and Fleet Street journalist, Arthur Machen. This was described by the author as "mere fiction and invention. My tale concerned the spirits of the great English bowmen of the old wars, summoned from their rest by St. George's mighty command 'Array, array, array!' But when the people began to talk about it, they called these good bowmen 'The Angels of Mons.' " By his own admission, Machen thought up the story after reading the premature account of British defeat at Mons in the Sunday papers. He said, "I know what we read and how we were sick at heart. And I suppose that in the first place it was to comfort myself that I thought of the story of 'The Bowmen,' and wrote it in the early days of September."

It is a mystery how this story could possibly be confused with the Angels of Mons. It spoke of Agincourt and bowmen and St. George. The true account was of Mons and horsemen and angels. The fiction was not even begun until September and not printed until the 29th. Reports of the angels began to be heard from August 25, with the *Evening News* keeping people well abreast of the facts throughout the following weeks. It seems that those who were skeptical of the possibility of Divine intervention tried to cause confusion to discredit the angelic reports.

The Reverend Peter Wright wrote to tell me about an elderly man who had been his gardener when he was rector of East Blatchington, Seaford, in the 1960s. The gardener had seen the Angels of Mons and used to describe them with the words, "their wings were tucked up." Another person who wrote to me said her friend's grandfather was a soldier who saw the Angels of Mons. Many times he had related his experience and always with awe in his voice.

Three and a half years later in July 1918, the Allied troops were exhausted following the continued, relentless fighting in France. In March 1918 the Portuguese had joined the Allies and in May the Americans decided to send troops. Owing to vigorous enemy action against the Allied lines to the north of Béthune, at La Bassée, heavy casualties had been sustained. Because of the local geography, the British were left in a pocket which was liable to be hemmed in, cutting off the men and equipment it contained.

The following again comes from Captain Cecil Wightwick Hayward's first-hand account in *This England:*

> *So tremendous was the reverberating crash of concentrated shell and high explosive fire, that it literally shook the ground and dazed us, though we were nearly three miles behind the front line. The unfortunate Portuguese were practically blotted out wholesale, thus causing a gap in our front line, through which the enemy began to pour in mass formation. The few Portuguese left came staggering through Béthune, having thrown away their equipment in a mad desire to get away from the hell behind them.*

*Shortly afterward they were followed by the British troops whose flank had been turned.*

*In Britain everyone was asking "Would the Germans get through to Paris?", "Would the Americans arrive in time to check the advance?", "Will the English ports be shelled shortly by German guns from the coast of France?" But then we remembered the "Angels of Mons" and once again the whole British nation was called to prayer. The American people were summoned to do likewise and united prayer went up from all the English-speaking peoples.*

An event then occurred which is similar to the Biblical account in 2 Kings 7 where the Aramean army was holding a lengthy siege to the city of Samaria, so that the population was almost starving. But God sent a message through His prophet Elisha that the siege would end that day. It seemed an impossible dream, but that same evening

*the Lord caused the Arameans to hear the sound of chariots and horses and a great army, so that they said to one another, "Look, the King of Israel has hired the Hittite and Egyptian kings to attack us!" So they got up and fled in the dusk and abandoned their tents and their horses and donkeys. They left the camp as it was and ran for their lives ... the whole road was strewn with the clothing and equipment the Arameans had thrown away in their headlong flight!*

Captain Hayward's account continued:

*The enemy shell fire, which had been largely directed against the shattered town of Béthune, suddenly lifted and began to burst on a slight rise beyond its outskirts. The open ground was absolutely bare of trees, houses or human beings, yet enemy gunfire and then machine-guns raked it from end to end with lead. We stood looking in astonishment. The sergeant beside me said, "Fritz has gone barmy, sir; what in the world can he be peppering the open ground for?" As suddenly as it started, the enemy's fire ceased and, in the complete silence, there rose a lark's trilling song of thankfulness. The dense line of German troops which had started to move forward to victory in mass formation halted dead. And as we watched, we saw it break! I saw my sergeant and his men standing on the edge of a shell-hole waving their tin hats, shouting, "Fritz is retiring!" Indeed he was. Before our astonished eyes, that well-drilled and seemingly victorious army broke up into groups of frightened men who were fleeing from us, throwing down anything which might impede their flight.*

*It was not long before my sergeant arrived with two German officer prisoners. The senior officer gave the following statement: "The order had been given to advance in mass formation, when my lieutenant said, 'Herr Kapitan, just look at that open ground behind Béthune, there is a brigade of cavalry coming up. They must be mad, these English, to advance against such a force as ours in the open. I suppose they must be the cavalry of one of their colonial forces, for see, they are all in white uniform and are*

*mounted on white horses.' 'Strange,' I said, 'I
never heard of the English having any white
uniformed cavalry, whether colonial or not.
They have all been fighting on foot and in
khaki, not white.' 'Well, they are plain enough,'
he replied, 'See, our guns have got their range
now; they will be blown to pieces in no time.'
We saw the shells bursting amongst the horses
and their riders, all of whom came forward at a
quiet walk trot, in parade ground formation,
each man and horse in his exact place. Shortly
afterward, our machine guns opened a heavy
fire, raking the advancing cavalry with a dense
hail of lead. But they came quietly forward,
though the shells were bursting amongst them
with intensified fury, and not a single man or
horse fell. Steadily they advanced, clear in the
shining sunlight; and a few paces in front of
them rode their Leader—a fine figure of a man,
whose hair, like spun gold, shone in an aura
round his bare head. By his side was a great
sword, but his hands lay quietly holding his
horse's reins, as his huge white charger bore
him proudly forward. In spite of heavy shell,
and concentrated machine-gun fire, the White
Cavalry advanced, like the incoming tide over a
sandy beach. Then a great fear fell on me, and
I turned to flee; yes I, an officer of the Prussian
Guard fled, panic-stricken, and around me were
hundreds of terrified men, whimpering like children, all running. Their intense desire was to
get away from that advancing White Cavalry;
but most of all from their awe-inspiring Leader. We are beaten. The German army is broken.
There may be fighting, but we have lost the war.*

*We are beaten—by the White Cavalry. I cannot understand."*

The report of Captain Hayward continues:

*During the following few days I examined many prisoners, and in substance, their accounts tallied with the one given here. This in spite of the fact that at least two of us could swear that we saw no cavalry in action, here or elsewhere at that time. Neither did any of us see so much as a single white horse, either with or without a rider. But it was not necessary for us to do so, the evidence of their presence had to come from the enemy.*

There was a further National Day of Prayer on August 4, 1918, the fourth anniversary of Britain's declaration of war against Germany. Following this, an Allied attack began on August 8, an advance which never ceased until the Armistice was signed on November 11, 1918. As at other times in British history, there has been unmistakable evidence of direct answers to National Days of Prayer, especially so when it is representative of the Crown, the Church and both Houses of Parliament.

# CHAPTER TEN

# *Angels at Bedsides*

 have received an unusually large number of accounts from people who have seen angels either just before going to sleep or having been woken up during the night. I have excluded any that could possibly have been dreams which are a different area altogether, involving the subconscious. Most accounts of night experiences start with explanations such as, "I was not asleep, but definitely awake and not dreaming . . . " In fact people always seem to be very sure that they were awake when they saw an angel.

This chapter also includes accounts of angels who have been seen by people in the hospital. Sometimes the angel has appeared to the patient, at other times to a visitor or member of staff, and sometimes to two or more people at once. In the case of ill people, I have been careful to omit any stories which might have been the result of confusion or hallucinations caused by the illness or medication. As far as possible, these are the reports of ordinary, sane people in their right mind.

In July 1991 Sara Hiam of Harborne, Birmingham, was in the hospital recovering from surgery. She was very poorly and feeling afraid. Suddenly she was aware of angels "encamped" on her bed and she felt the peace and protection of the Lord. Sara says, "I actually felt a hand in mine and knew the peace of the Lord all the more strongly." Something similar happened to Stella Grimstead in March 1992 when she was in the hospital in Weymouth after a car accident. One afternoon she woke up to feel someone holding her hand. Assuming she had a visitor, she opened her eyes to see who it was. No one was there, but the touch had been real enough and the peace she felt even more so.

Barbara Whiting was a patient in the hospital in 1983, being visited by two ladies who are frequently used by the Lord to pray for healing. As they prayed for Barbara she felt a cool, refreshing breeze blowing gently on her face. No windows or doors were open so she could see no explanation for it at the time. I have heard of a number of incidents where the unusual refreshing breeze is due to the gentle flapping of angels' wings. Sometimes the angels are seen, at others their presence is merely sensed.

After her visitors had left, Barbara managed to get out of bed to reach her jug of water. She says, "I then heard the *beautiful* sound of a choir singing extremely high. It was of a pure quality, which was simply amazing to hear. I knew there was nobody around with a radio on and, anyway, it was much too high and exquisite for it to have been made by earthly voices. I knew without doubt that it was a choir of angels."

Gillian Warren of Lewes, Sussex, was in the process of giving birth to her third child in 1975 when she had her angel experience. She was weary and disheartened after several hours of labor and little sign of progress. Gillian describes what happened next. "I saw the Lord standing, holding my baby in His arms. Surrounding His head and the upper part of Him were many angels hovering. They were translucent, of a rainbow quality, and this whole sight filled me with joy and courage. About an hour later I gave birth to a super daughter, Susanna, who has given us much joy."

A baby may successfully survive birth only to become seriously ill soon after. Such was the case with Richard Beardow who, at six weeks, was so ill that he was expected to die. The hospital doctor and both parents were standing around his cot, aware that Richard could not survive much longer. Just then his father, David, saw something like a light shadow passing over the cot. He felt peace, and the certainty that baby Richard would be all right. He told Wendy, his wife, "He will be OK now. We can go home to our other children." Wendy and the doctor were unconvinced, but David was completely sure that Richard would make a good recovery, which he did.

Elderly people are just as likely to encounter angels. Beryl Sisley's father was seriously ill in the hospital after a severe heart attack. He said an angel tapped on his pillow to get his attention and said, "You are not going to die." He recovered and lived another two or three years. This meant his daughter, a missionary in Rwanda, saw him again, the next time she was on leave.

One instance where a nurse and patient both saw an angel occurred in about 1960. Audrey Graham was a student nurse when, standing in the ward, her attention was caught by a rustling sound, like corn being blown by the wind. She saw an angel in the ward, looking gentle and kind, standing beside a bed. Audrey walked over and the patient said, "Don't be concerned, Nurse, I've just had an angel come to tell me I'm to be with Jesus tonight. The angel told me not to be afraid; he will help me through. When I get there, I will tell Jesus about you." Audrey continues, "Although I did not want to rob her of any part of that experience, I gently replied, 'Don't you think Jesus would already know of me?' Her face lit up as she said, 'Of course He will. I hadn't thought of that.' This lovely lady died quietly in her sleep that night."

Three people have told me of instances where someone visiting a hospital patient has seen an angel. Rose Williams, who now lives in Great Baddow, Essex, remembers an incident from forty years ago which occurred when her mother was very ill following a stroke during an operation. Rose was at her mother's bedside in the hospital, praying for her, when she was amazed to see an angel at the top of the curtain surrounding the bed. The angel had large white wings and was looking down lovingly at Rose's mother. In her hand she carried a staff. Rose was sure this meant that her mother would recover, although the doctors had given her very little hope. Contrary to medical expectation, her mother made an excellent recovery from both the stroke and the operation.

The second visitor was Philipa Dodd, who was at her father's bedside in Solihull, West Midlands. During what was his last night on earth, the family took turns to stay awake with him. At about 1:30 A.M. on Maundy Thursday, April 8, 1982, Philipa was keeping watch while her two sisters slept. Philipa reports, "I had been saying quiet prayers when I suddenly heard myself say aloud, 'God bless you, Dad, you're in the Lord's hands now.' Just then, I looked across at him. I knew he had taken his last breath and was at peace. Then for a few seconds I saw a yellow haze over Dad and angels moving upward, carrying him, it seemed up a stairway. My only regret was that my sisters were not awake to witness this event, at the time of Dad's death, and to feel the wonderful peace that took over the room. The sight of the angels thrilled me so much that on the card with the funeral flowers I wrote:

> God bless you, Dad;
> The angels came.
> I saw them there;
> They took you up the golden stairs.

In 1989 Peter Gathergood was with his wife in King's Lynn hospital visiting a handicapped baby who used to come and stay with them. As they sat by the baby's cot, Peter explains, "A porter wheeled into the ward a bed carrying a small, pale child with a drip in his arm. Behind him were a man and a woman, presumably his parents, both looking very worried. As I glanced up to take in this scene, I was at once aware of a shining white figure, about seven feet tall, standing beside the couple, looking down on the child. I instantly 'knew' this was an angel who had come in a protective and calming role.

"The curtains were then drawn around the bed," continues Peter, "and I never saw the little family again, but my lasting, considered impression of that snapshot scene is as real as I write this account as it was the day it happened. I have no doubt I saw an angel."

Florrie Shrubb was at home in Sittingbourne, Kent, when she saw an angel in the early hours of May 16, 1986. After weeks of being nursed at home, her husband was now fading away from cancer in the hospital. She woke up and sensed the presence of someone in the room. Florrie says, "Turning over, I saw, standing by my bed, a perfect angel with outstretched arms. She was clothed in celestial white, such as I've never seen before and I was enveloped with a wonderful sense of peace. As usual, I set off later for my daily visit to the hospital to sit beside my husband's bed. At 11:15 A.M. he passed peacefully away and I knew the angel had come to prepare me for this."

Marjorie Waine of Barnham, West Sussex, had also been nursing her husband during his illness of four years, following two strokes. In the early hours of February 26, 1968, she had fallen asleep on the bed beside him and was awakened by a rustling sound at her side. As she turned to look at her husband his head was being lifted from the pillows and she watched while his eyes opened wide and he gazed ahead with utter amazement and wonder. Then a smile lit up his face and his appearance was totally changed. All the marks of his illness and suffering were wiped away, and he looked radiantly happy. This is a man who had been desperately ill, unable to move, and who had been unconscious the day before.

Marjorie was so thrilled that in her delight she began to sing psalms. She glanced at the clock which showed seven minutes to four. The room was filled with light and joy and a great feeling of awe and wonder. Her face broke into a broad smile. "After about two minutes his soul flew joyfully away with the angel at whom he had been gazing. Then his head was placed gently back on the pillow and he stopped breathing. I could not help singing,

> *'The strife is o'er, the battle done;*
> *Now is the Victor's triumph won;*
> *Now be the song of praise begun;*
> *Alleluia.' "*

Marjorie says, "In the moment he was called, he was healed. The black blisters had disappeared from his legs and the blackness had gone from his feet. When I went to change his position, I could move him easily down the bed, whereas the previous day his fluid-laden body was too heavy for the district nurse and myself together to move in any way. In that moment of healing, he was young again, and as he lay there with a rapturous look on his face, he seemed to be forty years younger. What emerged so strongly from this unexpected experience was the tremendous power available to us, of which we are only scratching the surface. I realized that God can remove mountains and perform any miracle."

Someone who had an even more dramatic experience was Dorothy Kerin, the founder of Burrswood, a Christian healing center in Kent. Dorothy was eager to help others experience the healing ministry of Jesus after she herself was miraculously healed in 1912. She began to be ill from the age of twelve, suffering from diphtheria, pneumonia, pleurisy and tuberculosis, which weakened her so much that she was ill for many years and bedridden for the last five. On February 4, 1912, she received Holy Communion and asked her little sister, Evelyn, who was sitting with her, to sing the hymn "Abide With Me." Evelyn tried but did not know the words very well. Just then, both sisters heard it sung beautifully and distinctly from beginning to end by an unseen choir of angels.

For the next two weeks, Dorothy was blind and unconscious due to tubercular meningitis and there was no possible hope of her recovery. Yet on February 18, she saw a great light all around her and an angel took her hand, telling her, "Dorothy, your sufferings are over. Get up and walk." All the family and nurses were standing around her bed, certain that this was Dorothy's dying moment. They were all amazed to see her get out of bed unassisted and walk down the stairs. She asked for food and was offered milk in a feeding cup. She refused it, saying she wanted "real food." She walked unaided to the larder and got a meal of meat and pudding. Her astonished family watched her eat it all with great relish. Dorothy said, "How I enjoyed that meal. It was the first solid food I had been able to digest for years." The following morning, everyone was amazed to see that normal, plump, healthy flesh had replaced her previously skeletal figure and discolored skin, her condition for years. When the doctor arrived he asked, "Is it possible that this is the girl I left dying yesterday?"

Recalling the two weeks when she was unconscious, Dorothy described a vision she had of heaven. She had seen many angels there, some wearing haloes or carrying lilies. Some formed an altar and Jesus held a Communion cup and gave Dorothy a drink from it. Describing the angels she said, "Their movements made lovely music and they all looked as though they were coming and going with some definite purpose. No words of mine can exaggerate the exquisite beauty of the scene." Dorothy was twenty-three when this healing occurred. She went on to inspire many people to find healing through Jesus during her long and fruitful lifetime.

Leslie Harvey, who was then living in Bournemouth, had a comforting experience at home. He had been nursing his wife, Bea, for a long time and was lying awake in bed early one morning in December 1985. He became aware of an angel standing in front of him. He was dressed in a white cloak with soft folds that partly covered his head, so his face could not be clearly seen. Les watched the figure go upward, and was left with a tremendous feeling of peace and complete rest, which lasted throughout the last days and death of his wife two weeks later. Les was not a Christian at the time, but committed his life to Jesus a couple of years later, when he was in his late seventies. He is now a member of our local church, as is Ann Scriven, who describes her own experience. Several years ago, at a time when she was suffering regularly from nightmares, Ann woke up from a particularly horrible one. She sat up, but before she had time to switch on the bedside lamp, a bright golden light appeared at the foot of the bed. Ann says, "It was so bright that I closed my eyes. As I opened them again, I saw three angels in the center of the light. They were very close together, the one in the middle being the tallest, and they all had wings. I stopped shaking and watched them for a while. Then I closed my eyes again, and even though my eyes were closed, I sensed the light disappearing. When I opened my eyes again the room was in darkness."

Angelic encouragement of a different kind was given to a young man in Birmingham when he was severely ill. Connie Thorpe, headmistress of the local school, met him when she was taking harvest gifts from the school children to the bedridden at home. The young man's mother and grandmother continually wept about his illness, which was of no help to the patient. When Connie was alone with him he said, "I wish they would stop blarting [crying]. When they've gone to bed an angel comes and sits at the bottom of my bed all night. I think it's my guardian."

Another night vigil of protection occurred for Cynthia Davison who, in August 1988, was staying for a week at Taizé, a Christian community in France. She had always been terrified of the dark, so the long dormitory where she spent the nights in pitch darkness did not allow her much sleep. In addition, the lady in the bed opposite had nightmares, and most nights ran screaming from the dormitory, with Cynthia following to comfort her. One night, however, Cynthia managed to sleep after quietly singing to herself the words of a psalm: "In our darkness, there is no darkness, with You, O Lord, our darkest night will be as bright as day." Later, she woke during the night to find a glow coming from a white figure sitting on the floor between her bed and the lady who Cynthia thought of as Mrs. Nightmare. At first she thought the figure *was* Mrs. Nightmare, and spoke to her, but as she spoke, the figure disappeared, yet the light remained.

Cynthia explains, "I was not afraid, so I lay back and remembered how I had fallen asleep singing the psalm. It was the best night's sleep I have *ever* had. I realized later that it was the only night that Mrs. Nightmare didn't wake up screaming. I'm sure the figure was a guardian angel for us both. It gave her a peaceful night, and the glow gave me enough light to feel comfortable so I could sleep. What I find amazing to this day is that I wasn't frightened or even amazed. I just accepted that I'd asked for help and God had provided it. I don't understand it; I just know that it happened."

Mary Benford was also in need of encouragement in early 1991, as her son, his wife and their four children were preparing to emigrate to New Zealand. She knew it was the right move for them, but realized, too, that she would miss them very much. One night in bed she was trying to let the Lord be her sole source of strength, allowing Him alone to fill the gap that would be left by the departure of her family. Describing what she saw, Mary says, "Suddenly there appeared a young man standing by our bed and I knew immediately he was an angel. He had short fair hair and wore ordinary human clothes, but he was standing as if on sentry duty. I was not at all frightened, but did not know if I should speak to him, so I asked the Lord. He told me I could speak to him, but it was not necessary, as he was simply there, at the Lord's command, specifically to watch over my husband and me. This was not the sort of comfort I had been looking for, but the Lord knew it was the help I needed at the time, and the knowledge that the Lord watches over us has been very valuable."

Laura Wills of Chesham, Buckinghamshire, also required encouragement one night when she was having much pain and suffering with resulting sleeplessness. During this time, in the autumn of 1991, Laura was crying out to the Lord one night for His help. Several angels surrounded her bed, and a bright light shone through the bedroom door. She was puzzled by this, as she knew the door was closed and she had not left the passage light on. She wanted to see where the light was coming from, but feared, if she moved, the angels would go away. She said aloud to the angels,

"Please do not go away," got out of bed and opened
the door. The passageway was in darkness, so she returned to her bed. The angels were still there and the
light was streaming through the closed door. The angels stayed for several minutes and, when they had
departed, Laura knew the Lord had sent them. It reminded her of two Bible verses, "God is light and in
Him there is no darkness at all" (1 John 1:5) and "I
will be with you; I will never leave you nor forsake
you" (Joshua 1:5).

Irene Tomlinson of Poole was also lying in bed
one night in 1986 at a time when she had suffered a
good deal and required comfort. She became aware
of a tremendous flooding of warmth and reassurance
of God's love for her. Then Irene saw a heavenly being over her bed: "Two huge solid golden wings either side of a gleaming golden spherical head. The
smile was so full of softness, love and warmth that I
was left in no doubt that I had experienced an encounter with one of God's angels."

Ten years ago an angel came to Grace Tye of
Worthing. At the time, she had been caring for her
husband, who had suffered from senile dementia for
about twelve years. One night she was suddenly
woken from sleep and she saw the whole length of
the wall facing her glowing with a radiance beyond
description. The brilliance blocked out the furniture
and mirror completely. An angel then stood beside
her bed, bending with his arms toward her, and a
lovely warm glow enveloped her. He was tall with a
beautiful face, golden hair and no wings. The loose
sleeve of his white robe showed his wrists, and Grace
bent to kiss the wrist nearest to her. At that moment
the angel vanished as silently as he had come. The
wonderful light went out, leaving the room as dark as

before. However, the warm glow Grace felt inside remained with her.

Back in 1919 Blanche Hill was caring for her brother, Joe, who had returned seriously injured from fighting in World War I. At their home in Woodend, Warwickshire, Blanche had gone to bed for a short nap. She heard her name called and opened her eyes quickly. At the bottom of the bed was a gleaming white angel with wings that nearly touched the ceiling, and he lit up the room. She felt he would help her look after Joe, and with that he disappeared. Blanche was certain of the angel's unseen assistance each day after that. The story was sent to me by her grandson, Anthony, as she is no longer living. Anthony heard her tell this story many times, always exact in every detail, and considers it was perhaps the most important thing that ever happened to her.

Catherine Muir also has strong memories of the angels who visited her one night in 1959 when she was eight years old. Brought up in Scotland she had been used to hearing Bible stories read to her by her mother. One night, when she was in bed, she saw a figure in the doorway and, assuming it was her mother, said, "Hello, Mummy." "There was no answer and the figure came nearer, so I saw it was not my mother. I rubbed my eyes, but it was still there. I was not afraid, but full of wonder. Gradually the person seemed to multiply with about five identical figures forming a circle at the foot of my bed. I felt privileged to see such a thing and did not want them to go away. When they gradually faded, I felt sad that they had gone. I have not told many people about this, but I once heard someone else, who did not know of my experience, describe seeing an angel become a circle in just the way I saw it."

Another eight-year-old who saw angels was Ruth Knight. She had been asleep and woke up to find two white-clothed angels looking at her. One of them said, "We're not ready for you yet." She saw them clearly and remembers looking up at them.

I think the reason why so many people have seen angels in their bedrooms is two-fold. Nighttime can be a lonely and frightening time, when problems of the day become exaggerated and out of proportion. It is, therefore, often the time when we are most in need of protection and encouragement. Secondly, if God wants to communicate with us, we may be rushing around too busily in the daytime, with too much on our minds, to notice Him. Perhaps we need the stillness of the night to hear what He wishes to tell us.

# CHAPTER ELEVEN

# *For the Skeptic*

**W**hen a remarkably similar event happens to totally unrelated people in different parts of the country, even in other countries, it can only, I think, be genuine. I have already given examples in other chapters of comparable experiences, but the similarities between the stories I have collected together here are particularly striking. Recently, I was talking with an agnostic and the subject of my research into people who have seen angels came up.

He said, "You mean visions of mystical spirits."

"No," I replied, "actual angels, with real bodies and striking faces, and sometimes with huge wings and powerful swords."

The agnostic replied, "I've never heard of that; I can't believe it could be true. Tell me what someone has actually told you they have seen." I shared with him some of the following experiences, which he found convincing.

In 1982 Patricia Stewart was carrying her eighteen-month-old son Richard down the stairs at their home

in Yorkshire. Richard was a baby who required constant attention; he did not sleep much and Patricia
was exhausted. As she went to walk down the stairs,
she tripped on the top step and, unable to regain control, toppled to the bottom. As she was falling,
Patricia was aware that she was heading for the glass
door at the foot of the stairs. She then felt two arms
catch her and stand her upright with Richard still in
her arms. Surprisingly, she did not feel at all shaken,
and Richard did not cry or seem upset. Patricia often
used to pray to God for angels to protect her family
and she felt sure this was a clear demonstration of
that care.

Someone else caught in mid-fall was Susannah
Tilly, who lives in Littleover, Derby. Susannah had
already had several miscarriages and in 1988 seemed
likely to lose the baby she was expecting. After
twelve weeks of lying in bed and resting, she felt she
needed a break and persuaded her husband to take
her for a short outing to the shops.

Susannah explains, "I felt very shaky on my feet
and, as I came out of the butcher's shop, I slipped on
some grease on the step and fell. Had I landed hard
on the step, I am certain that would have finished my
pregnancy. But, as I fell, I felt very strong hands grab
my arms and something which felt like a soft cushion
placed under my bottom. I never hit the ground but
was firmly stood on my feet again. I looked round to
thank whoever had helped me, but no one was there.
Suddenly the word angels came into my mind and I
was conscious of their presence.

"The next day," Susannah continues, "a member of
our church home group came to visit us and I shared
with him what had happened. He said that on the
evening previous to this incident, when the home

group met they had all felt that they should pray especially for me. They sensed that I would be in danger during the following day! It was certainly a dramatic answer to their prayers."

Skeptics sometimes question whether angel experiences only happen to those who already have faith and who are therefore predisposed to believing that what they have seen is an angel. This is certainly not the case, as several of the people who have written to me are not Christians, although some have become Christians as a result. Examples of this are given in Chapters 5 and 13, and here is another.

Katie Bridger was on a double-decker bus going to work in Kent on October 24, 1991, when the brakes failed. She was sitting upstairs, at the front of the bus, so she had a clear view as the bus hurtled out of control toward a brick wall. As a Christian, she instinctively prayed for the safety of everyone on the bus. As she did so, she saw several angels who put up their hands to stop the bus, just before it would have hit the brick wall. The amazing thing was that, although the bus stopped very suddenly, no one was thrown forward as would normally happen—it was as if the bus had been stopped very gently.

When Katie saw that on the return journey the bus had the same driver, she mentioned to him that she had been on his bus that morning. The bus driver was so amazed that they had been brought to such a gentle sudden halt, that Katie told him about the angels she had seen who had prevented the crash. As a result of this miraculous escape, the bus driver became a Christian.

Katie's account is a living example of the promise in Psalm 91:9-12: "If you make the Most High your dwelling, He [God] will command His angels concerning you, to guard you in all your ways; they will lift you up in their hands, so that you will not strike your foot against a stone."

Something very similar happened to Bruce Humphrey in January 1985 when he was traveling in New Jersey in America. He was driving a large Cadillac, accompanied by his wife, two other passengers and a large quantity of luggage—a heavy load. Even on three-lane dual highways, in some places cars in America are allowed to cross the opposite highway to reach the other side of the road. So Bruce was not surprised to see a van turn to cross over the three lanes on his side of the road to pull into a parking lot. However, another car at that point was coming out of the parking lot and was blocking the entrance, so the van and car met nose to nose and both stopped. Between them they blocked all three lanes entirely. Bruce knew a crash was inevitable, but he changed lanes quickly so that the impact would be lessened by his hitting the fronts of both vehicles, rather than the side of the van. He braked hard, but was certain his car could not stop in time. Miraculously, however, he stopped just short of the blockage. At the speed at which they were traveling, there should not have been enough stopping distance, especially considering the added weight on board. Also, on such a busy highway, it was fortunate that nothing else was coming alongside when he rapidly changed lanes. Another thing which surprised Bruce was that none of the passengers or himself were thrown forward in their seats or felt any movement at all when the car stopped so suddenly. All four agreed that unseen angels had brought the car to a sudden, yet amazingly gentle halt, in an impossibly short time, thus preventing a serious accident.

Three elderly people in different places also had similar experiences to each other. Sybil Fellowes, who is in her eighties and lives in Croydon, fell over as she was walking along the pavement. She tried three times to get up but could not and there was no one around to help. She prayed, "Lord, I can't get up; please help me." She explains, "At once, two lovely young men stood by me. Their faces were so full of joy and peace that I knew they had come from heaven. They stooped and took my arms and stood me on my feet. I turned to thank them but they were not there." The same verses of angelic protection from Psalm 91 also seem relevant here.

About seven years ago Vera Stephens of Bolton fainted as she was getting out of bed wearily one morning. She saw an angel with a lovely serene face gently lift her up by holding her left arm. Another angel helping on her right side had an equally serene, yet different face from the first.

In the early hours of October 14, 1991, Margaret Pugh's 88-year-old mother got up to go to the bathroom. When she returned to bed she sat on the edge for a moment, but slipped to the floor. She was unable to get up, not having the strength in her arms or legs to pull herself up. She crawled to the sofa, hoping to be able to drag herself up, but to no avail. In desperation she prayed, "Dear God, please help me to get up." The next thing she knew she was standing up, facing her chair. She has no recollection of the transition from floor to standing. She and Margaret were both sure an angel had helped her.

Two other strikingly similar incidents involve people at the roadside. One Sunday in 1987 Zena Farlowe and a friend, Mary, were visiting York for the first time. Zena's son was competing at a bowling

club, so they dropped him off and decided, during the
time he was there, to attend the service at the Church
of St. Michael le Belfry. As the church is in the city
center, they had difficulty finding a place to park and,
after driving around and around, eventually found a
space several roads away from the church. They
found the church and enjoyed the service, but afterward could not remember where they had parked
their car. An elderly man in a tweed suit appeared
and offered to help. They said they couldn't find their
car and he gave precise instructions for which they
thanked him. Walking quickly for several minutes
and following the instructions exactly, they thankfully
found their car, but then needed to find the way in the
unfamiliar city to the bowling club to collect Zena's
son. The elderly man had not followed them, but he
suddenly appeared again and inquired if they needed
help once more. He asked where they were going and
again explained exactly which route to take. They
had a very easy journey, following his directions. The
gentleman's assistance had been so timely on each
occasion that Zena and Mary have remained convinced that he was an angel. In strange surroundings,
they felt they had been ably looked after by the Lord.

Another family, the Fiddimores of Cheltenham, were
driving to Wales Bible Week at Builth Wells. On the
way, they all noticed an elderly man with an angelic-
looking face at the side of the road. He had a walking
stick and he waved at them. Twice more, several miles
apart, exactly the same thing happened: they saw, at the
side of the road, the same man, who waved and smiled
at them. As they drove into the town of Builth Wells,
just by the roundabout, they saw him again. He gave
them a "big happy smile" and waved his walking stick
in greeting. They all felt blessed by this experience and

were sure he was an angel, encouraging them that they were going in the right direction. Their journey was unbroken and it was not possible for this man to have been in four different places along the way, unless he had been traveling by helicopter, which seems most unlikely.

Two miraculous escapes from serious injury on the road bear many similarities. The Reverend David Rushworth-Smith, who in his early days as a clergyman was not able to afford a car, was riding a motorcycle. He set off at about 9:30 P.M. one snowy night in the winter of 1953, after speaking in a little church at Kersey in Suffolk. The conditions were dangerous as it had snowed heavily and was now freezing. As David was proceeding carefully along, the road seemed suddenly to slide from under him and he shot across to the right-hand side, straight toward a pile of hard ice. He says, "I was all alone, miles from anywhere and knew that if I hit the ice and was hurt I could freeze to death. In a split second, I prayed for help and I saw a strong pair of large hands take hold of the handlebars. They picked up the bike, with me still on it, while it slid across the road, almost on its side. The hands put the bicycle and myself back on to the crown of the road, still going forwards. The hands did not leave me until I was quite balanced again, and they disappeared as suddenly as they had come."

David Rushworth-Smith made an interesting observation when he said, "Angels tend to be shy creatures. They are messengers and do not flaunt themselves. If at all possible, they do not appear." This could explain the incident described in Chapter 2 where the steering of a motorbike traveling on a moorland road in thick mist, was taken out of the hands of the driver, Harry Thompson, just as he

approached a hidden hairpin bend. In that event, the
assistance was as clear as in David's case, but Harry
did not see the hands, only felt their intervention.

Something comparable happened to Arthur Harvey
in the early 1960s as he was driving home from work
in Basingstoke, Hampshire. There was plenty of traffic as it was rush hour. Arthur describes what happened: "Suddenly from a side road on my left came
a car across my immediate path. I recall slamming
the brakes on. The next thing I knew I was driving,
somehow, the wrong way down the side road from
which the car had come. I pulled over to the side of
the road and stopped."

Arthur continues, "Many times I have returned to
the scene. Not only did I miss the car directly in my
path, but I also missed a traffic island. I've checked
it out—physically and mechanically I could not have
steered the car round that corner, and I was not aware
of any skid. Also miraculously there was no on-
coming traffic, at the busiest time of the day, when I
was on the wrong side of the road. I certainly believe
an angel was responsible for the steering in this situation."

In July 1992 Dorothy Frosdick went to an
11:15 A.M. Holy Communion service at her local
church in East Hoathly, Sussex. Her thoughts were
drawn to her friend Deane, who had recently died in
the hospital. She was thinking how much Deane
would have enjoyed the choice of hymns that morning. Suddenly the whole church was full of angels,
praising God and filling the church with glory. With
them was Deane, looking radiant. She was not one of
the angels, since they are entirely different beings
from humans and we do not become angels when we
die. Deane was not dressed like the angels and was

clearly not one of them, but for this occasion was accompanying them. It encouraged Dorothy greatly to see this glorious sight.

A similar sight was experienced by Inger Denniston at a meeting for prayer and praise at St. Andrews, Chorleywood, the church she attends in Hertfordshire. As they were worshiping, she suddenly saw the whole church full of angels. They joined in with the worship and Inger saw among them her father, whose funeral she had attended in Norway the previous week. Again, he did not look like the angels, proving that people do not become angels, but he *was* part of the praising throng. He looked so happy to be there. Inger was thrilled when Andy Gardner, another church member sitting next to her, whispered, "Look, the whole church is full of angels praising God." After a short while they disappeared, leaving Inger with a wonderful reassurance, particularly since Andy had confirmed what she had seen.

Appearance of angels, both in the Bible and today, are seen most commonly by only one person. It therefore adds more credence to the experience when more than one person sees the angel or angels at the same time, as in the above example and in the following accounts.

During the worship time at the New Life Christian Fellowship in Sunderland in 1989, Stephen Poxon heard an extremely high, crystal clear voice join in with the worshippers. There were no words, but a strong, beautiful sound. Without mentioning this to anyone, Stephen was very surprised and pleased when his host for lunch, Frank Talbot, asked if he had heard particularly high singing during the time of worship. They both felt certain this sound was very much higher than a human voice can reach and must have belonged to an angel.

About thirty years ago, Doris Baker and her daughter, Margaret, were walking through Govilon, near Abergavenny, on their way home. Margaret, then aged fifteen, saw the angels first, poised above a hedge. As her mother came up to her she said, "Look at the angels." Doris looked up and saw the wonderful sight of three large angels, pure white against a deep blue sky. They were close together, positioned in formation. Both Doris and Margaret were rendered speechless for a few minutes, but when they found their voices again they discovered they had seen exactly the same thing. They were greatly encouraged by this vision which they have never forgotten. At the time they had been experiencing some opposition from Doris's husband about their going to church and felt that maybe that was why they had received this special gift. Doris now says, "I shall never forget this outstanding experience."

Norina Penny and her family of two adult daughters live in Bournemouth. One evening her younger daughter, Nadine, went to visit her ex-boyfriend, Kenny. He was in some distress and needed someone to talk to, but as he was also liable to be violent, Norina was concerned for her safety. A few minutes later Norina and her elder daughter, Claire, decided to go for a walk. They stopped by a church and Claire suggested they pray for Nadine. During the prayer, the word "angel" came into Norina's mind. "I knew instantly that I must pray for one of God's angels to protect Nadine, so I prayed with Claire for an angel to come."

That night Norina slept peacefully, even though Nadine had not yet returned home when she went to bed. The following morning Norina went downstairs and found Nadine asleep on the settee. She woke up and said, "I saw an angel last night." Her mother asked, "When?" Nadine replied, "About twenty minutes after I left the house." Claire then came downstairs and her mother asked, "What time did we pray for an angel last night?" Claire replied, "About twenty past eight, about twenty minutes after Nadine left." Nadine said it was like a bright light in the shape of a person. She knew instantly that it was an angel sent to protect her, and it had then disappeared into the mist.

In 1983 Peter and Sue Pimentel were shocked by the news that their unborn baby had been diagnosed as having spina bifida. The hospital suggested strongly that they consider a termination but they did not want to do this. When the diagnosis had been confirmed, Sue lay on her bed in great distress, but heard God clearly say, "Trust Me." After about two weeks they decided to spend time praying with a couple of friends specifically for the situation. To start with they were unsure what to pray for, but then the whole atmosphere changed and they felt a tremendous feeling of glory, deep joy and a great welling up of praise. Sue felt uplifted and saw the whole room filled with light and angels who were praising God. One of the others, Marion Bird, saw a very large angel, who seemed to fill the room, standing directly behind Sue. He had large wings which were wrapped around Sue. The overwhelming joy that they felt was due to the strong sense of God's presence, and was not brought on by the sight of the angel. They all knew, without a shadow of doubt, that the baby within the womb had been healed of spina bifida.

The sight of the angels had just confirmed what everyone had felt, that God had healed the baby.

Throughout the rest of the pregnancy, none of the doctors, or anyone else who had not been part of that prayer meeting, could believe that the baby had been healed. They continued to talk about the baby as if it would have spina bifida. When she was born, completely normal in every way, Peter and Sue called her Jemimah which means "dove," the symbol of God's Holy Spirit.

An angel experience always has a lasting effect on the person who receives it. Doris Wake, who saw an angel over seventy years ago, told me, "All these years I have lived with the knowledge that I have seen an angel—nobody can shake me." Marion Delfgou of Loughton says, "I have not previously shared my angel experience, except with my family, and have felt rather shy about doing so. But now I wonder why we should hide so much that is wonderful. Angels are part of God's kingdom—the Bible is full of them." There are, in fact, 300 references to angels in the Bible and their activity is mentioned in Bible readings, hymns or prayers nearly every week in church.

Moira Salman, who saw an angel as a child, says, "I was not imagining it and I have never had any mental illness. I firmly believe in what I saw, but not many people believe me and therefore I do not talk about it much."

A seven-foot angel stood by Joyce Nott's bed, holding her hand, while she was having a heart attack. Doctors and nurses were busily trying to save her, and the pain was too severe for her to speak. "I remember thinking, 'So this is what dying feels like.' In my mind I cried out, 'God, help me.' Through the warm, loving hand I felt holding mine, and the sight of the shining angel, I know that God answered my prayer for help. That experience has changed me. I have lost my fear of dying."

Two women, who had similar experiences of being helped by angels on either side of them and Jesus Himself, were both feeling rejected and unloved at the time. Elizabeth Johnson of Lancaster, in her first year at college, was in her room feeling lonely. After crying and soul-searching, she prayed for God's help. Elizabeth says, "I then felt very peaceful and sensed an angel at either side of me and one in front of me and Jesus's presence above my head from behind. A message came to me: 'Angels are ministering spirits sent by God to those He loves.' This made me feel as though God loved me and thought me special, to let me have such an experience." Pauline Ravenscroft, of Croyde, Devon, had been badly treated by some people and was feeling rejected. This made her feel reluctant to go to church, although she had previously enjoyed going. Many times she set off, but turned around at the church door and could not bring herself to go in, so went home instead.

Pauline explains: "One day after suffering it for many months, I cried to the Lord to help me with this problem. I heard the church bell ringing and the Lord told me to start walking up the road to church. About sixty yards from church, as I was walking along, I was praying in tongues [a heavenly language, given by God]. I was suddenly aware that I was not alone. To my left and right I saw two men dressed in white, with large red crosses on their robes. Their hands were held high, holding swords aloft. I also knew that there was someone walking behind me, and in front of me was a person with a white robe and long wavy hair. I knew that He was Jesus, and I remember thinking that I must not walk too quickly or I would tread on His robe.

"I was escorted up to the church door and taken inside," Pauline continues, "and when I sat down the angels and Jesus stood in front of me. What a way to be taken to church! I felt such joy and peace and excitement. When the service started they faded from view, but I knew that spiritually they were still there. I was no longer afraid, and could hardly wait for the end of the service, so I could tell the rector and some close Christian friends. They were delighted to hear my news.

"What the Lord was showing me," Pauline reflects, "was that I must not be afraid of anything, because He is with me in every situation. The following day He spoke to my heart. 'I know that you have been suffering and I have allowed these sufferings to make you strong. I sent you my angels, and I came myself, to strengthen you so that you would have victory in Me and give the glory to Me.' This was such a blessing."

The effects of such an event are long-lasting. Vicki Stafford, whose angel experience is related in Chapter 5 says, "The gift of an angel is not something anyone could take lightly. I cannot analyze away the reality of the experience—it has added to the texture of my life. Those who know me well comment on a change in me."

# CHAPTER TWELVE

# *Angels versus Demons*

ngels are God's SAS, His special army of soldiers. They are usually invisible to us but they are constantly on active service doing God's will. Evil is present in many forms in our world today and one of the angels' vital activities is to help protect us from the effects of evil. Satan used to be one of the chief angels in Heaven, equivalent to the Archangel Michael. He became proud, wanted more power for himself and disobeyed God, so he was expelled from Heaven (Revelation 12:7–9). Since then, he has continued on earth seeking ever more power for himself. Satan is also called the Devil, Lucifer and the Evil One, since he was the originator of evil (Genesis 3). He took with him many followers from among the angels. Satan organizes his army of "fallen angels" to oppose God and His people. His army is described in Ephesians 6:12 as "the powers of this dark world and . . . the spiritual forces of evil in the heavenly realms." But Jesus "disarmed the powers and authorities . . . triumphing over them by the cross" (Colos-

sians 2:15). In Luke 10:18 Jesus said, "I saw Satan
fall like lightning from heaven."

Jesus was subjected to intense suffering on the
cross to defeat sin and death. As one who was sinless
Himself, He knew that only His death could atone for
everyone, otherwise we would all have to die spiritually and be separated from God forever. Because Jesus had not sinned, His sacrifice was sufficient. The
worst part for Him was the separation from God the
Father, while He took our sins on Himself. He told
Peter that He could have called down "twelve legions
of angels" [over 72,000 of them] to rescue Him from
the cross (Matthew 26:53), but He chose to take our
sins so we could be forgiven.

Jesus never watered down the message He came to
proclaim, so Satan angrily wanted to destroy Him. But
he could not have the victory, because Jesus is supreme.
The angels' power is greater than that of humans, and
they are not limited as we are by space or time; they
can go anywhere, instantly. They are especially available to help those who are in a situation from which
there appears to be no way out. However, unlike God,
they can only be in one place at a time.

A word of warning: we must never worship angels.
They neither deserve nor desire it (Revelation 19:10
and Colossians 2:18). Our worship must be reserved
for God alone. Neither should we seek after visions
or appearances of angels. Those who have seen angels are not more spiritually mature, nor do they have
more faith than those who have not. If, for some reason, God wants you to see an angel or a vision, then
you will. It is not something we should worry about
or pursue. It will happen if it is meant to. In fact,
seeking after visions can open up a person to the
power of Satan, because he can counterfeit visions

and give false revelations. Some people have told me of "angels" who have appeared in black or surrounded by darkness. These are not from God, because "God is light; in Him there is no darkness at all" (1 John 1:5).

The "occult" is a satanic counterfeit of God's true supernatural powers and includes the following: witchcraft, magic, ouija-boards, séances, levitation, consulting mediums, fortune-telling, including tarot cards and horoscopes, astral projection, meditation in yoga and seeking psychic powers. People who have been involved in the occult can sometimes be overtaken by immense fear, which can control their lives, or by repeated nightmares, which prevent normal sleep. In specific situations, this can threaten to attack them physically, as well as emotionally and spiritually. Kim Spicer was living in East London opposite the house of a medium and was conscious of a real sense of evil. Kim says, "I didn't like this and prayed for protection. God put a tall angel as a guard in front of my house. He was dressed in white, was very brilliant and carried a sword which he held up in front of him."

Tim Prevett, of Wool, Dorset, used to be heavily involved in horror books and films and frequently enacted role-playing games. These are fantasy, but encourage the participants to take on the role, thoughts and ideas of the characters. When the characters are evil, the effect can be long-lasting and damaging. These negative influences terrified Tim at times and led him to seek an answer in Christianity. When he became a Christian, he realized that horror films and role-playing games were damaging so he abandoned them. Since then, he has several times been aware of an angel standing beside him as a guard, or of many angels forming a protective circle around him. Tim says, "These angels are not like the types seen on Christmas cards; they are like warriors. Very tall, seven to eight feet, very muscular and they always have large drawn swords. As soon as I am in an oppressive situation, I pray and become aware of angelic protection. Then I feel very peaceful and can face up to the fears that were imprinted into my memory from my involvement with horror and roleplaying."

Christine Buckley had suffered abuse from other people throughout her life; she was both a battered baby and a cruelly treated child. She had also been adversley affected by her own dabbling in the occult as a teenager. She says, "A wonderful Christian couple prayed for me, rebuked Satan's hold over me, and anointed me with oil [a symbol of God's healing]." With the miraculous change that came about in her life, Christine knew Jesus's care for her and the truth of the Bible came alive. One night in February 1983, when she had been a Christian for a few months, Christine awoke from sleep to be confronted by a vision of "ugly horrible demons prodding me with pitchforks as if they hated me. Then came a fantastic vision of thousands of angels with swords, fighting my battle. I can fully remember them being about twelve feet tall, in brilliant white with kind, shining faces, radiantly showing God's love and authority. I had a wonderful sense of peace, protection and safety."

A retired clergyman, the Reverend George Measey of Worthing, told me about a time in 1947 when he and two others were conscious of angelic protection. They had been praying for someone and had seen an evil spirit cast out. They were then themselves at-

tacked by the evil spirits—an experience so terrifying
that George asked God never to let it happen to him
again. The three of them together said the Lord's
Prayer and when they came to the line "Deliver us
from evil," the atmosphere changed. George says, "I
heard the sound of angel voices in glorious unison.
The experience was heavenly, uplifting." That evil
spirits cast out of someone else can enter into others
is warned against in 1 Peter 5:8 "Your enemy the
Devil prowls around like a roaring lion, looking for
someone to devour. Resist him, standing firm in the
faith."

One night, in December 1991, Norah Threader was
alone in a hospital room unable to sleep. She was
praying for various friends and relatives and picturing
their faces in front of her. Then the faces distorted
into horrible gargoyles, like Halloween masks, which
terrified her. As a Catholic, she prayed to St. Michael
the Archangel to defend her from these creatures
which looked so evil. "Suddenly," says Norah, "there
stood St. Michael, eight feet tall, wielding a huge
sword from left to right, as if it weighed no more
than a feather. At his stroke, all the horrible creatures
disappeared. Then he opened his wings slightly and
gestured to me to go behind him. Then he closed his
wings around me, sheltering me from all the evils of
the world. I knew then I was safe."

Not long ago, Whittenham Clumps near Walling-
ford, Oxfordshire, had become the focus of Satanist
activity. Christians in the area heard that a group of
Satanists were planning to go there on Hallowe'en
1990 to celebrate a sinister ritual and to give the high
ground to Satan. Some Christians therefore met there
earlier in the day to walk around the highest clump
and to dedicate the area to God. At one point they

stopped walking to pray and sing. While they were praying, one of them, Christopher Wyatt, heard very high, choral-type singing. It sounded like thousands of beautiful voices singing in perfect harmony, much higher than human voices. When he shared the experience later with others, he discovered that some of them had also heard angelic singing on other occasions, which convinced him that that was indeed what he had heard.

Gill Page lives in Aldershot, Hampshire, an area which has been used for a great many witchcraft activities, causing a sense of oppression in the area. Preparing to lead a Bible study in the church she attends, she was led by God to use a particular Bible passage which she realized would present a clear challenge to the people there. Gill explains: "During the night before the Bible study was to take place, I awoke in real fear. The room seemed full of evil; it was almost stifling. Unable to move, due to the oppressing fear, I called out the name 'Jesus!' Then the door opened and an angel came in—a figure in long robes, bathed in brightness and carrying a small light. The angel came to my bed and opened the drawer of the bedside table, placing the light in the drawer. With the words, 'There, you will be all right now,' the angel left the room and I fell into a deep sleep. The next day I had no concern over my message, only an assurance that God wanted me to share it, even though Satan had tried to stop me.'

Charles Murray of Leeds had a strange experience when he woke one morning. He continued to lie in bed awhile, enjoying the warmth. His imagination exaggerated his thinking until he found himself indulging in most selfish and harmful thoughts. The more he struggled to free his mind from this increasingly wild imagination, the more forceful it became until he seemed to be part of a battle. Charles says, "When I felt I was losing the battle, I heard a loud voice outside myself, as if someone was in the room. The voice spoke clearly, with authority, saying, 'Go home, there is nothing here for you.' The reply to this command was a loud howl of infuriated rage. 'Aaarrgh!' It was so fierce that it made my hair stand on end. The command was repeated, 'Go on, go home.' The response was the same, but fainter and more distant, until I was finally left in peace. I am convinced that these were the voices of an angel, protecting me, and a demon, who had no good intention for me, and was trying to attack my thought-life. This was not my imagination; I know it was a reality. I hope such a thing never happens again and I thank God for His love and mercy in sending an angel to protect me."

Sarah, an eighteen-year-old from Merseyside, grew up in a home where there had been a great deal of evil activity. She and her sister, who is two years younger, are Christians, so they have God's protection in the home. Sarah once asked God to show her anything in her bedroom which was not of Him. She was very frightened when she saw dozens of pairs of eyes all around the room, looking at her. Then she asked God for protection and was shown a very strong-looking angel whose arrival made all the strange eyes disappear, never to return. Sarah says, "I have seen a certain angel twice. He is well built, like a body-builder or a bouncer! He has wings which are folded down, so they almost can't be seen. The first time he appeared with a fanfare trumpet, which he lifted up and blew. The second time he held a flaming torch out toward me. I touched the torch with my hand and I went numb all up my arm and into my body. I felt I was being blessed by the Holy Spirit, to help me in my Christian life."

Another eighteen-year-old, Tim Comley of Bristol, was involved in evangelism—that is, talking about his Christian faith to others. One night he was awake, not dreaming, when he felt a great sense of evil. He panicked and was very afraid. Then inwardly he called out to Jesus and was reminded of Psalm 34, "The Angel of the Lord encamps around those who fear Him and delivers them." This kind of fear is the awe-inspired reverence God's followers show toward Him because of His great majesty. It bears no relation to the frightening fear which is connected with evil. As this psalm came to Tim's mind it was as if the evil oppression had been dissipated like a pin pricking a balloon. Although he had not seen the angel, the sense of an angel taking care of the situation was very real, and the evil was dispelled completely.

During her teens and early married life, Dora Smart, who lives near Crawley, Sussex, had suffered much at the hands of others. Her marriage was blighted by her husband's heavy drinking and sometimes she felt quite desperate. She is now eighty, but one summer's night, about forty years ago, she woke in terrible pain at three o'clock in the morning. With all her ill health and constant tiredness she felt sorely inclined toward suicide. She resisted the temptation, however, because she knew this thought was put in her mind by Satan, and her two sons needed her love and care.

Dora then felt the walls and ceiling of the room coming in on her and saw blackness. She shouted, "My God," and, with that, the blackness, ceiling and walls retreated. Then Dora felt a warm caress over her face and, looking up, she saw a large gold and silver wing. She knew then that angels were with her and that God has greater power than Satan. Dora felt a great peace within and much of the pain was taken away. This experience led her to seek God in prayer and Bible study and join the church; it showed her a great awareness of God's love.

Nicholas Maguire from Southport was lying on his bed one evening when he saw black shadows flying around above him. He pointed at them commanding, "In the name of Jesus, be gone." It was as if lightning came from his fingertips and hit the shadows, so they departed. Then a white shimmering human figure, about eight feet tall, stood next to him. Nick says, "Realizing it was one of God's angels, I said, 'Hello' and put out my hand to shake hands. A white mist gathered around my hand as I felt the angel shake hands with me!"

On May 13, 1969, Ann Atkin of Rye, Kent, recorded in her diary an amazing series of encounters. She and her husband, Ron, had been affected by a woman who was trying to dominate them with black magic. She was staying in their home and sleeping in their guest room, next door to their bedroom. Ron and Ann were both woken up at about 2 A.M. by a bumping noise coming from the guest room. Then Ron was alarmed to see thick rods, about one foot in diameter coming down from the ceiling into him. He was shaking all over and felt oppressed by evil attacking him. He shouted, "Get out," over and over again and hummed a carol, desperate for protection. Ann wondered what was happening to him, as she could see nothing, though she heard bells tinkling. Ron said he saw lots of sheep around the bed; they had tinkling bells around their necks.

With the sheep was a donkey and some angels in

the form of shepherds, who came up to his right side.
At the same time, from the left-hand side, darts were
coming at him, snake-like objects. The shepherds re-
pelled them, and Ron thanked them for their help.
They responded and one put out his hand, which Ron
reached out for and held. The shepherds had their
feet on the floor, wore simple brown cloaks, and the
most striking thing about them was their strong-
looking foreheads.

While the shepherds and sheep were all still
around Ron, Jesus appeared from above, off the
ground, holding a full-sized crook. He gave the crook
to Ron who, after holding it for a few moments, returned it to Jesus. However, He had meant Ron to
keep it, so He gave it back to him. Jesus disappeared,
but the angelic shepherds and sheep remained. Ron
felt happy and, all at once, had a great feeling of
peace. He drew strength from the crook, which took
away all fear.

Ron had never had any strange experiences or visions before. The whole thing was like an experience
of spiritual rebirth, giving him for the first time a
strong belief in Jesus. Having been wide awake for
four hours, he got up at 6 A.M., but could still feel the
sensation in his hand of holding the crook, and a tin-
gling right up to his elbow. He could feel it in his
hand for the next three weeks, although it was not
physically there, but holding the crook had a perma-
nently calming effect on him. The experience totally
changed Ron and affected all areas of his life. As a
person, he began to find God important in his life. As
an artist, his style changed completely. As an art
teacher, he had much greater understanding and dis-
cernment. He felt the strength of Jesus, through the
crook, remaining with him. He and Ann broke off all

contact with the woman using black magic, sensing the damaging effect she could have on them. A few nights later, Ron was surprised to see two angels with huge, powerful wings come to his bedside. He felt that perhaps they were there to encourage him in the changes being made in his life, since the amazing experience a few nights before.

Something equally unexpected was experienced by Nigel Parry during the night of April 19, 1991. As a Christian himself, Nigel had been encouraged by his best friend who had also become a Christian the day before. Maybe this is why Nigel was harassed by evil, as a counterattack. He was staying the night on the floor of another friend's room, but as he was lying there he felt the physical weight of an evil force pressing down very heavily on him. He felt choked, swamped; it was so real and awful. It was not a dream, but an actual physical force. Nigel prayed desperately to God for protection, and eventually slept, but woke during the night to see a figure in the room. The figure crouched down, with his hand on Nigel's chest, praying for him. Nigel knew it was just what he needed and, following the silent prayer, he slept peacefully. The next morning his friend said, "I had a weird dream last night, I felt I was being strangled by demons." He described the oppression he had felt in his dream and Nigel told him of his own terror, which was no dream, but very real. Then Nigel said, "Thanks for praying for me in the night." His friend replied, "What do you mean?—I didn't pray for you." Nigel told him about the figure who had touched his chest and brought him such peace. They discussed whether it was an angel or Jesus Himself, who had rescued him from being harassed by an evil force. Whoever it was, Nigel knew it was a direct re-

sult of his prayer for God's protection before he went
to sleep.

Andrea Bond lives in a village in Wales which is
currently an area of witchcraft and oppression. She is
a prayerful person who has been greatly concerned
about the effect of occult influences, especially on the
teenagers in the area, including her own. In 1991 she
was praying at home beside an upstairs window,
when she suddenly saw the sky full of golden angels.
It seemed a mass of gold, very protective and encouraging. A few months later Andrea was in a downstairs room, again praying for the area. Looking out
of the window, she was amazed to see hosts of angels, on foot, marching past. They were all facing
one way, resolute in their marching. They wore armor, with their strong breastplates being the most significant part of their attire. Again Andrea felt that she
was not alone in the battle against evil and praised
God for sending this huge army.

Satan and his "fallen angels" deceive people with
evil thoughts and may use disaster and illness to
damage our trust in God. This is exemplified in the
story of Job in the Bible who, in spite of countless di-
sasters, causing him to become very ill and to lose
everything, nevertheless remained faithful to God.
The whole book of Job results from Satan's direct attempt to shake his faith in God (Job 1:6–12 and
2:1–7). We meet evil every day and the Bible does
not minimize the power of Satan in the world. Satan
tries to distort the truth and influence someone to the
extent of taking over their personality. Angels, however, bring encouragement and assistance promoting
faith and reliance on God. The power of God is far
stronger than the power of Satan and God will ulti-
mately triumph over him. Anyone affected by Satan's

activities and power can be released by Jesus's power, which is far stronger. Jesus can cleanse and restore, giving blessings to outweigh by far the suffering due to evil. I know people for whom this is certainly true. Joel 2:25 says, "I will repay you for the years the locusts have eaten ... you will have plenty to eat until you are full, and you will praise the name of the Lord your God."

# CHAPTER THIRTEEN

## *Angels and Men*

Without wishing to sound sexist, I had not expected many men to respond to my request for information about angels. This is partly because men tend to be more reluctant to let their thoughts and feelings be heard, especially if the subject is likely to be doubted or laughed at. Women, in my experience, are more inclined to put pen to paper, whereas men often intend to reply but never quite manage to do so. This is not just my opinion, since several men have asked me how many of their sex have responded, specifically for this reason. Statistically, too, it is known that women respond to polls and questionnaires more readily than men. For example, the BBC receive a much larger proportion of correspondence, whether complimenting or criticizing programs, from women rather than men. I have therefore been surprised by the considerable number of men who have written to me about angel experiences. They are from all walks of life, from doctors to car work-

ers, scientists to bishops, and come from all parts of
Great Britain, as well as abroad.

Almost all of the respondents have begun their letter with comments such as "I was very heartened to
read your request . . . ," "I have told no one about
this experience, not even my own family, because it
may invite ridicule, but I do welcome the opportunity
to share it with someone . . . ," and "I feel I should
share my experience with you."

Frank Duryea, who lives in New Jersey, America,
wrote about an incident which occurred in July 1990.
Frank was scheduled for a knee replacement, and was
due to be in the hospital for two weeks. In forty-five
years of marriage, Frank's wife, Jane, had never been
alone at night in the house so Frank was feeling concerned for her, as well as for himself with the impending surgery. Frank writes, "The night before I
was to enter the hospital, I knelt in prayer and asked
God for His strength and protection. I then climbed
into bed and, out of the corner of my eye, I saw a figure standing in front of the window, on my wife's
side of the bed. I immediately got out of bed, with
my fist clenched, ready to punch this intruder. Then
I noticed that he was dressed as a Roman guard, and
stood there with his hands at his sides with an aura of
gentle peace about him. Suddenly I had that calm and
peace too. I climbed back into bed with the certainty
that Jane and I would be all right. I believe God, in
His love and mercy, sent an angel to minister to me
in my time of doubt and uncertainty." Needless to
say, all went well.

During World War II, Gordon Smith was at
Blandford Army Camp in Dorset. One evening he
visited the town of Blandford, where he fell into conversation with an army trainee who was in need of

both spiritual and financial help. Gordon felt it right to help him by giving him some money. This, in fact, was the last of his own money, so Gordon had to walk back to the camp alone that dark night. As he was walking, Gordon passed an old man he had never seen before, who said to him, "Are you Gordon Smith? The Lord told me to give you this." He gave Gordon a ten-shilling note, which was a great deal of money in those wartime days. Before he could even thank him, the old man disappeared! There was nowhere he could have walked off to in that space of time; he had just vanished.

Such behavior is a common sign of angelic activity, as I've noted elsewhere. The person seems perfectly human and normal until they disappear without trace. Then it is apparent to the observer that they have "entertained angels without knowing it," as it says in Hebrews 13:2. Gordon was rewarded with far more money than he had given to help the trainee, and he knew that God had sent that angel, in the form of an elderly gentleman, to encourage him. His sudden disappearance convinced Gordon that he was an angel.

A similar experience occurred, in 1981, to Terry Low, who, although only a curate, was in charge at Longfleet Parish Church in Poole, Dorset, there being no vicar at the time. One night, the churchyard was vandalized with curbstones kicked out and many crosses broken and thrown down. The next morning Terry was sadly surveying all this wanton damage not knowing what to do, since he was unsure if it had been caused by bored vandals or by a Satanist group. Just as he was wondering where to start, a man came and stood beside Terry and said, "Don't worry about all this, it will be all right. Next Sunday, get half the congregation out here to pray while the other half are praying in church. You don't need to be anxious about it." Terry felt reassured and comforted. He turned to reply to the stranger, but there was no one there. A church worker was cutting grass nearby, so Terry asked him where the man had gone. The gardener said, "I saw you talking; I assumed you were praying," but he insisted, "There hasn't been anyone else here." Terry knew for certain that he had not imagined it because he remembered the man's voice. He also knew that the gardener could not have been the stranger, because he had heard the noise of the mowing machine being used in the background throughout his conversation and, anyway, their voices were not at all similar.

The following Sunday, before the service began, Terry told the congregation that he intended to go out into the churchyard to pray and anyone who wanted to do likewise should join him. The rest could remain in church. Terry went outside and exactly half the people followed him. They prayed in each corner of the churchyard. As a result they overcame their previous feelings of grief and dismay about the destruction. Those remaining in church also had a special time of prayer and the church service which followed was very powerful and uplifting. It took a working party and members of the families owning the damaged graves to repair the destruction, but everyone in the congregation was much more peaceful and accepting than they would have been without the visit and advice of the angel.

Prebendary John Collins told me about another incident where an apparently human helper suddenly disappeared. John and his wife, Diana, were on vacation in South Wales, about a year after they were

married. At the time they were swimming in a bay
that was known to have strong currents. The sea was
quite rough so they agreed not to go out of their
depth, even though Diana was a capable swimmer.
As a poor swimmer himself, John did not go beyond
knee-depth. However, he was alarmed to see that, almost as soon as she began to swim, Diana was being
carried rapidly out to sea. John says, "I shouted but
it was impossible to make myself heard against the
wind. I looked round desperately. There was a beach-
side cottage in the distance. Should I run for help or
would it be too late? Should I go in after her or
would that only make the problem worse?

"At that moment," John continues, "I saw a young
man running along the beach at the edge of the sea.
Before he reached me, he seemed to have grasped the
situation and dived into the waves. With powerful
strokes he reached Diana and pulled her back to the
shore. As soon as she was in her depth, I went to
help her and then turned to thank the young man, but
he was nowhere to be seen. As it was a very long
beach, he would still have been easily in sight, even
if he had run off quickly in either direction. He had
not said anything, and the way he disappeared without trace made me believe we had seen an angel. He
had certainly prevented a tragedy, just like it says in
Hebrews 1:14: 'Are not all angels ministering spirits
sent to serve those who will inherit salvation?' God
sometimes sends angels, in the Bible and today, to
protect His people in physical danger."

Harry Knight, who lives in Ongar, Essex, has had
more than one experience of angels which, as I've
said elsewhere, is unusual. In Harry's case the events
were years apart and both, as in all angel experiences,
were totally unexpected. The first is recorded in

Chapter 5, the second comes from an extract in his diary for January 30, 1983. He wrote, "At 5 A.M. I had been awake for about an hour, with great concern for Ann [a Christian friend of the family]. I had been praying in tongues [God's gift of a special prayer language] for quite a while, asking God to ensure her a peaceful release from pain and anxiety, which Ann herself had been earnestly asking God for. After a few quiet moments the most beautiful singing and music began. It was so positively definite, so absolutely real. The orchestra had the most magnificently beautiful and expressive instruments played in perfect harmony. The quality of the harmonized singing in many parts was way beyond anything I'd heard before. Then suddenly it stopped. I woke my wife and told her in detail of this heaven-sent utter beauty."

Someone else who unexpectedly heard an angelic choir was Ken Barnatt, who lives in Ferndown, Dorset. He told me about it the very week it happened, at the beginning of March 1991, just after I began researching into angels. Ken has a key for his local church office, so had gone there alone one evening to do some photocopying for a Christian group he leads. As he came out, he heard the most beautiful singing. He thought it must be coming from the church, so he went to investigate, but the building was silent and in darkness. He found no one else around. The singing lasted for about a minute, and Ken was left feeling amazed and privileged to have heard it.

The sound of angelic singing has come in all kinds of different situations, some of which have been described in Chapter 7. On the evening of December 28, 1990, it was heard by Dr. David Lewis, a university lecturer and author living in Turnbridge Wells, who immediately wrote an account of what happened. The previous month he had the opportunity to lecture at a Russian university and, while there, was introduced to members of a Russian organization which invited him to visit some of the remote peoples of northern Siberia. While contemplating this visit, on that particular evening in December, David was prayerfully considering some of the peoples of the Arctic regions of Russia, such as Yukaghir, Yakut and Chukchi. These are peoples who, as far as he knew, had been neglected by the Christian missions. Suddenly he became unexpectedly aware of beautiful worship music in a wonderful crescendo of heavenly praise, rising up to ever greater heights. In Genesis, the first book of the Bible, the Tower of Babel had become a symbol of man's own striving for selfish power. As a result, God had confused speech so that, for the first time, many languages were spoken. As David heard this great sense of oneness in worship, it seemed as if the effects of the Tower of Babel were being reversed, as all human languages gave way to one language of praise.

David says, "I also understood from this experience that helping the unreached peoples of this world actually affects the worship of heaven itself. The music and praise I was hearing seemed to be getting progressively higher and more exalted. My impression was that these high registers of singing could not possibly be human and had to be angelic."

The sight of a traditional-looking angel conjures up different emotions. John Laing, a factory worker at Vauxhall Motors, Luton, had an unforgettable experience late in 1961. He had recently joined a Christian fellowship group which met in the lunch hour, because he was seeking God, although he was not yet a Christian. At about twelve o'clock, as he was on his way to the group, John had popped into the lavatory. On one wall he was startled to see an amazing figure appear, standing quite still, with a bright shimmering light surrounding it. He said it was large, with the appearance of an angel and he was awestruck for a while by the sight. This proved to be a conversion experience for John, because afterward he became a Christian.

The vision Stephen Baker saw, on the other hand, was a sign of protection for other people, although seeing it certainly blessed him too. He and his wife had been praying about their son-in-law who was working as a police officer in a part of Bristol where it was difficult to maintain order. It was becoming so threatening that, for the safety of his family, he was seriously considering resigning from the force.

One morning, while he was praying for his son-in-law, Stephen had a vision in which he was looking down from a height on to the house and small back garden belonging to his daughter and son-in-law. On each of the two rear corner posts of the garden fence stood enormous angel guards, each holding a sword which they pointed toward the center of the garden. Stephen knew at once that the problem had been solved. He had to go away that day, so his wife phoned their daughter to ask how things were. The daughter replied, "Well, they're better," and only then did her mother tell her about the encouraging vision her father had seen. This showed that God had the situation in hand, using His angels to protect the family.

Sydney Loader, the verger of St. Peter's, Yateley in Surrey, also saw a vision of angels in church, in about 1960. At a midweek Holy Communion service,

about twelve people in the congregation had gone up
into the chancel area of the church and were kneeling
at the altar rails ready to receive communion. As
Sydney was praying for them, he noticed a golden
light around the priest and people, and then the whole
chancel was filled with beings in golden light. Sydney remembers, "The chancel screen had gone and I
could see these figures wore long robes, down to
their ankles. I could see their feet, and they had
strong determined expressions on their faces. That
part of the church was filled from the floor to the
high roof, and they moved steadily, weaving to and
fro. Then in an instant they were gone. The ancient
wooden screen was again visible and the church was
back to its usual appearance."

When the Reverend Ray Jones was a chaplain in
the Royal Navy during the Falklands War, he prayed
that his home would be filled with angels protecting
his family. During that time one of his sons, who was
at Exeter university, brought a friend home. On entering the house, the friend declared, "I sense the presence of angels in this place." He had known nothing
of Ray's prayer.

John Noble is a regular speaker at Spring Harvest,
a Christian convention held each Easter. One year at
the Prestatyn Spring Harvest, John and other leaders
were walking around among the congregation during
a time of worship to God. With five thousand worshippers, the times of praise and worship are always
special, sometimes including singing in tongues.
However, on this occasion, John suddenly became
aware that the singing had moved into an altogether
higher plane. John remembers, "There was a strong
sense of God's presence and the sound of the singing
seemed to swell to a great crescendo, echoing around

the tent as if we were in a cathedral. After some minutes the sound subsided and we were back to normal
Spring Harvest praise which is always a blessing but
hardly out of this world. I consulted with a number of
other responsible people who could only explain the
phenomenon in terms of an angelic accompaniment."

The great-grandfather of Margaret Shepherd, the
Reverend William Mayo, did not himself see his angel protectors but was told of them later by others.
He was returning alone one night from taking the
sacraments to a dying man. Two unemployed men
lay in wait, expecting the clergyman to be unaccom-
panied and intending to rob him. They were therefore
surprised to see two other men with Mr. Mayo, one
walking either side of him. Some time later, one of
the men who had been to London in search of work,
returned home to Salisbury. He found that Mr. Mayo
had been helping to support his wife and family in
his absence. This made him feel guilty, so he confessed to him that he and a friend had intended to attack him, but had been prevented by seeing two other
men walking with him. Until then, Mr. Mayo had
known nothing of his heavenly companions of that
night.

A similar event occurred in about 1926 to the
grandfather of Frank Lloyd, who wrote to me from
Tamworth, Staffordshire. His grandfather was pit
manager of the local mine. Smoking below ground
was strictly forbidden because of the danger of an explosion which would risk many lives. One miner had
been brought before Frank's grandfather twice having
been caught smoking, but was allowed to continue
with his job when he promised not to smoke again.
Now he had been caught once more and Frank's
grandfather had no option but to sack him. He did

this sadly, since he knew the hardship it would cause the family.

Frank Lloyd describes the outcome: "The following Sunday my grandfather was preaching at a Methodist village chapel over the hills, to which he traveled on horseback. It was dark when he rode home, and all the way he was wondering how he could help the miner who had lost his job. By the time he got home he had a plan. He asked my grandmother to take a message to him the next morning, asking him to come to the pit. When he arrived to see my grandfather the following day he looked very contrite. He was offered a job at the pit-head which would not involve him going underground. He accepted gladly.

"The miner turned to go, but turned back saying, 'I want to make a confession and, when I have, you may not want me working here. I knew you were preaching over the hill last night, and I guessed you'd be on horseback. I hid with my twelve-bore shotgun and I was going to shoot you.' 'Well, why didn't you, then?' asked my grandfather. The miner continued, 'I always thought you went on your own to go preaching, and I never thought your horse could carry two, but just as you came into view and I was about to shoot, I saw the other chap in a white coat behind you on the saddle. I'm sorry that I ever thought of doing such a thing.' My grandfather insisted that he had been alone on the horse but, to his dying day, the miner swore there were two men on the horse that night."

Fred Lemon frequently gives his testimony of how Jesus and two angels came to visit him in prison. On the night of August 10, 1950, alone in his cell, he woke to find three men standing in front of him. Fred swung his legs out of bed and sat bolt upright on the edge, wide awake. The man on the right said, "Fred, this is Jesus." The man in the middle to whom he pointed then spoke to him. Clearly, yet gently, He traced the whole of Fred's criminal life up to the desperate present. He knew everything about Fred, just as He knew the woman at the well of Samaria, so that immediately He met her, He was able to recount all of her past (John 4). Fred listened to every word, surprisingly not afraid or overawed in this unusual situation. Jesus showed Fred that God was offering him forgiveness for every wrong he had ever done, because of Jesus's death. This paid for Fred's sins and His rising to life again to overcome the power of death. At the end of that wonderful talk, Jesus said, "If you want to become a Christian, you must drive hatred from your heart." Fred knew He spoke the truth, and that He referred to his attitude to the prison warders, toward some of whom he had felt extreme hatred, to the point of contemplating murder.

Fred had been listening with his head in his hands but, as the last sentence was spoken, he looked up. The three men, still facing Fred, were fading through the wall. There was a distinct click and he was gone. "That was Jesus Himself, here in this cell," Fred told himself. There was no fear, instead he lay down in great peace and slept. This experience understandably changed Fred completely, so he has gone on to lead a fruitful, joyful life.

The Reverend Dr. Denis Ball, who had a Christian teaching ministry through the Arts and Teaching Services Trust, had an angel experience thirty-nine years ago. Soon after his marriage, Denis and his wife, Florence Mary, were unable to find accommodation together, because of financial hardship. Denis was able to afford lodgings near his work in London, but the room was only large enough for a single bed, so Florence Mary had to go back to stay with her mother in Bournemouth. Denis was unhappy with this arrangement so, one evening after the rest of the household had gone to bed, he decided to spend time on his knees before God, seeking a solution. Denis describes the scene: "I selected the kitchen for the occasion and knelt in the center of the room, resting my elbows on a wooden chair. The bare light above me gave the room a clinical look and I closed my eyes to shut it out. I felt very alone and wondered why my wife and I had to go through this time of confusion. 'What are You doing with us, Lord?' I cried. The words had no sooner left my mouth when I became conscious of being surrounded. If someone were to relate to me this incident which I am describing, I would ask a multitude of questions. As a matter of fact, I did ask many that night. Who were these magnificent beings? Were they real or imaginary? Why had they come—to me?"

Denis continues, "As I silently sought for answers, it dawned on me that I was not at all afraid; astonished, intrigued, but not afraid. My eyes were still closed—I had not thought of opening them. But now I took a deep breath and slowly opened my eyes. They were there—angels! I could actually see them. There must have been ten or twelve of them all around me in a regular circle. The kitchen had grown in size for their circle was reasonably large but they were in no way confined. In height they were nearly seven feet, and each stood in an attitude of utmost confidence and rest, hands clasped at the front and faces looking down on me kneeling there. They were such beautiful and dignified beings and the only way

I can describe their faces is to say that they glowed
with a golden sheen which radiated the wisdom and
the knowledge of the ages. They were timeless. As I
gazed into their eyes, I had a distinct feeling that I
was looking into another world. I cannot even ade-
quately describe their robes, for they were much
more than coverings for the body; rather, they
seemed to be expressions of their character, vibrating
with life and purpose. Indeed, the whole company of
them gathered there that night transformed the
kitchen into a powerhouse. But why had they come?
I seemed to absorb the peace of these wonderful beings; I was protected. Then, quite suddenly, I found
myself outside the circle as an observer. I could see
myself still kneeling with my arms resting on the
chair while the angels stood guard around me. I remembered that "angels are sent to serve those who
will inherit salvation" (Hebrews 1:14).

"As I continued to watch, another change took
place. An almost impenetrable darkness was seen to
cover the angels, but this darkness could not draw
nearer, nor could it penetrate an invisible dome-
shaped canopy suspended over them. Darkness had
met with light but darkness could not overcome it
(John 1:5). At this stage I could see nothing of what
the darkness held, but I could feel it in my spirit as
a dark, hideous deception which sought to devastate
me and to divert me from the course approved by
God. Gradually I perceived their grotesque forms and
I noticed that some were darkly beautiful: they were
more devious in their attack. But I took courage, and
hope rose within me, as I noticed that at no time were
the angels distracted from their task of watching over
me. Not a tremor shook them as these powers of
darkness sought access to my kneeling form through

the circle of protection. Florence Mary and I were safe; no matter what trials and tribulations would come our way, such as finding a place to live or making ends meet, we could be assured that if we walked God's perfect way in His strength, no powers of darkness could touch us."

The men whose experiences I have related here are all sane, sensible men who have honestly told what they saw and felt. Their accounts disprove my original assumption that men are more reticent to allow their deeper feelings to be shared.

## CHAPTER FOURTEEN

# *Angels Abroad*

ll of my research has been carried out in Great Britain, but some respondents have told me about incidents that happened to them while they were abroad. Others have written to friends in other countries whom they knew had had angel experiences, and they in turn have written to me. This chapter therefore contains a variety of experiences which have happened to both men and women, young and old, in various parts of the world.

Janice Rowland and her friend Lori were in France in July 1991 when they had an angel experience. They had spent a few days packing up Jan's belongings as she was leaving an apartment in Paris and returning to live in England. Jan says, "The little van was packed the night before we left, with not a spare inch of space remaining. A desk top, and the pictures and oil painting Lori had carefully wrapped would be loaded on the roof rack in the morning, as vandalism was rife in that area of Paris. Since we had an 8:30 A.M. ferry to catch at Le Havre, we rose at

4 A.M. As best we could, we lashed the roof load down with stretchy 'octopus' cables, although the job of hoisting it up and securing it was very difficult. Not only was it still dark at 4:30 A.M., but the roof was higher than we could conveniently manage."

Jan continues, "Finally, as heavy rain began to fall, we were on our way when, after about forty minutes, we heard the 'tap-tap-tap' of a hook come loose on the roof. Immediately I pulled over on to the hard shoulder and we both leapt out to inspect the problem. Imagine our surprise and horror when we looked up and saw absolutely nothing on the roof except a few cables! We looked at one another with disbelief and then got back into the van out of the rain. How could we possibly have lost such a heavy load without hearing it fall? Had we caused an accident? How far back was it, and how could we retrieve it on a motorway? The thoughts were racing through our minds when Lori said, 'Let's pray. Lord, what should we do? Please help us.' As a result of the prayer, I felt I should back up the van a bit to see if we could spot the missing load.

"After a minute or two Lori saw in her side mirror a large black parcel lying in the road. Suddenly a very tall man appeared next to it and she screamed, 'Hurry, someone's trying to steal our stuff.' When we arrived at the spot, he had moved the load to the side of the road. We both looked to see where he had come from; a car, a truck, anything he could have used to get to that point of the motorway, but there was not a vehicle in sight. Offering to help," explains Jan, "he lifted the long, heavy bundle, placed it back on the rack and, with a clothes-line Lori had found, he secured it neatly with intricate knots. When he had finished, Lori handed me a hundred-franc note to

give him, which he tried to refuse, but I insisted as
we were so grateful for his help.

"As we slowly pulled away from the side of the
road, Lori looked back to see where he would go. He
had disappeared; there was no sign of him anywhere!
The motorway was empty and the high embankment
would have been impossible to climb. As the truth
began to dawn, we started to laugh, and Lori
quipped, 'What do you think an angel will do with a
hundred-franc note?' We were the last ones to board
the ferry and, eight hours later, when we were back
in Lori's flat in London, the phone rang. It was
Mintie, a friend, phoning from Jerusalem. 'What happened this morning?' she asked. 'The Lord woke me
at 6 A.M. [5 A.M. Paris time] and I felt compelled to
pray that angels would protect you.' Shortly after that
another friend George, called in to ask what had happened that day. He told us that the Lord had laid on
his heart to pray for us all through the day."

Auriol Kenyon, who now lives in Birmingham,
wrote to tell me about another roadside incident experienced by her and her family in New Zealand in
1988. Their car had broken down as they were driving through the mountains in searing 120-degree
heat. Auriol explains, "We decided to pray for help
and, as a result, our son became convinced that the
next person who came along would help us. Sure
enough, very soon a young man with a truck came
along and he stopped. Without saying anything, he
unwound a rope and tied it under our bumper. He
towed the car up the hill with my husband at the
wheel, while the children and I walked."

But then the truck driver totally disappeared, the
truck included! Auriol's husband said the young man
had turned around and driven back down the hill.

However, Auriol and the children were walking up that way and he certainly did not pass them. There was no other way back down the mountain, as there was a sheer drop at one side of the road and a high cliff on the other. Another interesting point is that he spoke very few words to them, but he smiled all the time. They were all sure that God had sent an angel to get them out of that difficult situation.

Nineteen eighty-eight was also the year in which the Marfleet family were helped by an angel. At the time, they were in Irian Jaya, Indonesia, where the father, David, was a pilot with the Mission Aviation Fellowship. The eldest son, Peter, was eight and had been ill for several months with two tropical diseases, malaria and filariasis, neither of which were responding to treatment. He suffered repeated high fevers, severe headaches and nightmares during the little sleep he managed to get, and not only Peter but also the rest of the family were being seriously affected by his illness. It seemed that Peter was constantly reinfected, so the expectations of healing had not been fulfilled and Peter was feeling very discouraged. One evening David and Mary prayed three specific things for their son: that he would sleep well without nightmares or headaches, that his faith would be encouraged and that he would not be reinfected.

That night Peter did indeed sleep well but at one point he was woken up by someone. He thought it was his younger brother Jonathan, with whom he shared a room, but Jonathan was still fast asleep in his bed. The person trying to wake Peter was a boy about his age. He was dressed in white and looked European, rather than dark-skinned like the local people. Peter said, "He was not shining, just ordinary and he had a lovely face. He was swatting mosquitoes around my bed and I was awake, not asleep, when I saw him. I knew he was an angel and I felt very pleased he had come. I was very tired and I closed my eyes and went to sleep, so I didn't see him leave." This event coincided with the beginning of Peter's healing, and Peter has always remembered it as a very special event in his life.

Another missionary who suffered from repeated attacks of malaria was Naomi Cooper who has been a teacher in Luapula, Zambia, since 1987 with her doctor husband. Despite taking all the right medicines and sleeping under a mosquito net, Naomi seemed to go from one attack of malaria to another. Malaria is like a fierce flu with raging fevers and severe headaches. Sometimes it is accompanied by vomiting and diarrhea and the permanent weakness leaves one feeling depressed. Naomi says, "With no grandparents at hand to help with our two children, Jonathan and Ian, a husband very busy looking after all the sick people in the village and other missionary colleagues equally busy with their own jobs, I was more often than not out of action needing someone else to leave what they were doing to help me. I longed to be on my feet again but God was even closer at these times as I had more opportunity to pray and read the Bible. During one of the more severe attacks, I could not read or lift my head off the pillow, but in my mind I was singing to God. Suddenly, singing with me was the whole host of heaven, thousands of angels singing in perfect harmony, and it was wonderful! Had I joined them or they me? I cannot tell but I will never forget the wonder of it." This was a definite turning point for Naomi, both physically and spiritually.

In 1991 Leon and Paula Hoover, from Georgia, America, went, with their children, for a West Africa

Life Course in Burkina Faso, to prepare them for working as Bible translators in Togo. They lived as the only white family in the village of Yendere, which was the first time non-Africans had ever stayed in the village. Leon had been repeatedly ill, and at a later date was diagnosed as having two tropical diseases, giardia and malaria. After several nights of little sleep in the hut they were lodging in, Leon and Paula prayed specifically for a good night's rest. Following several hours' peaceful sleep Leon woke and thanked God for answering that prayer. Then he saw in the hut a man who was very much taller than any of the men in the village.

Leon says, "He wore a tattered shirt and trousers, like the men wore when working in the fields. I didn't see or hear him come in but he was sitting quietly on his heels at the foot of our beds. We had closed the door and window to keep the bats out, but he had opened the door, so I could see him in the moonlight. 'It's good you are sleeping well,' he said. 'Yes, I'm very grateful,' I replied. He was African in appearance, but spoke in English. In his big hands he held a gourd bowl, and he produced a large metal spoon. As he slowly stirred the contents of the bowl, I began to wonder just what was going on. I didn't recognize the man, but his whole manner suggested he was very pleased. He said, 'We were on our way from the beginning [presumably the beginning of my illness] but there was some trouble.' 'You mean there was a fight?' I interrupted. 'Merely a delay,' he continued. 'There was some opposition to our coming, but that's settled now. We're here and you'll sleep well.' "

This all sounds rather strange, but actually the same thing happened in Daniel chapter 10. Daniel had been praying and fasting because very discouraging news had come from his homeland while he was in forced exile in Babylon. He was praying to know God's will on the matter. After exactly three weeks an angel appeared, telling him, "Do not be afraid, Daniel. Since the first day that you set your mind to gain understanding and to humble yourself before God, your words were heard, and I have come in response to them. But the Prince of the Persian kingdom resisted me twenty-one days. Then Michael, one of the chief princes, came to help me because I was detained there with the King of Persia. Now I have come to explain to you what will happen to your people in the future." The Prince of the Persian kingdom is thought to mean a territorial spirit of evil oppressing Persia, and Michael is the Archangel Michael.

Leon explains, "When I first saw the man, I had wondered why his presence had not startled me. Now, however, it was obvious he was God's messenger. No more words were needed. He dipped the spoon into the bowl and held it to my lips. The liquid did not have much taste, but it seemed familiar. I woke Paula and my children, Luke and Natalie, and we sat on our beds in a semi-circle around the visitor. He gave a spoonful to Paula but I was concerned that Luke and Natalie would not drink, so I said, 'Each of you needs to take this.' He gave them each a spoonful, dipping into the gourd and putting the spoon to their lips. I watched them lie down again and, turning back toward the man, discovered he had gone, leaving as quietly and peacefully as he had come. In the morning I described the angel's arrival to my family. They had seen nothing, just as sometimes happened in the Bible where only one person saw an angel. For example, 'I, Daniel, was the only one who saw the

vision; the men with me did not see it' (Daniel 10:7).
It was in the recounting that I realized what was in
the bowl; it was filled with faith. The angel had been
sent to give each of us an extra measure of faith to
face the difficult times just ahead of us, beginning
that very day. The best part for me is not that I saw
an angel, but that God has given me a much greater
understanding of His holiness, and the faith He gives
us if we accept His will, even in the most trying circumstances."

This also brings to mind an instance in the Bible
where an angel was sent to feed Elijah, the prophet. He was exhausted having "run for his life" because he was being pursued by someone who wanted
him dead. Despairing and all alone, Elijah collapsed
by a tree and slept. "All at once an angel touched
him and said, 'Get up and eat.' He looked around and
there by his head, was a cake of bread baked over hot
coals, and a jar of water. He ate and drank and then
lay down again." This was repeated and, following
his two heaven-sent meals, Elijah walked a very long
distance, for forty days, without needing any more
food (1 Kings 19:3—9).

In 1964 a missionary college lecturer in Sierra
Leone, Win Bairstow, had to travel from the Eastern
Province to the capital, Freetown. Win recalls, "It
was a hazardous journey, over appalling roads and
frightening bridges. To cope with the various languages on the way, I took two of my students with
me; they were very keen to accompany me as they
had never seen their capital city. Before setting out
we prayed, asking for God's guidance and protection.
At one point, we were traveling down a straight road
when a tall African flagged us down. He was wearing
flowing white robes, such as those worn by some of

the Africans. The students said, 'Don't stop, Miss Bairstow.' But I did stop. There were three surprises about the encounter. Firstly, he spoke to me in perfect English, which was unusual in the bush. Secondly, he had no vehicle and a man so educated would have had a car. Thirdly, for miles there was no village or dwelling where he could have come from and it was very strange for someone to be alone. The man warned me that at the end of this road I would turn right to cross a river. It was not obvious, but the bridge had been damaged and I should be careful to find the safest place to cross. I thanked him and drove on and it was just as he said, but with the students' help we negotiated the bridge without difficulty. It did not occur to me that he was an angel until, some time later, I read Billy Graham's book *Angels—God's Secret Agents*. When I wrote to one of the students about it, he replied that they had discussed it at the time in the back of the car in the Mende language, unknown to me, and were both convinced that we had met an angel."

It is interesting to note that angels seem to appear as African in Africa, as oriental in Asia, quite different from the European-type of angels which appear in Britain. In heaven the angels are always in their heavenly form, but they can take on any human appearance necessary when bringing a message to us. Susan Dillon of Skelmersdale wrote to tell me she had seen huge, white angels with wings, swords and shields, taller than the tallest trees. She also described friends' experiences in other countries. Her friend, Jane, is working in Uganda and has met a man who has seen three angels with an African appearance. He described them as large, powerful, awesome beings. They told him precise details about what would hap-

pen locally and internationally and everything has
happened as they said. They warned of the famine in
Ethiopia, the war in Somalia and the spread of AIDS
in Africa, all before they happened. Another of Susan's friends, Kyoko, who lives in Japan, has seen an
oriental-looking cherub, who has given her warnings
about what she should avoid in her personal life. He
has Japanese clothes, wings and longer than usual
ears, a sign of a heavenly spirit in Japan. Kyoko has
found his visits a great help.

Alison and Tom Donachie were called by God to
go to teach English in China, so they moved there in
1988. They lived in the town of Shihezi in Xinjiang,
in the north-west of China; there were no other white
people in the town. Alison writes, "We had a three-
roomed flat in the college where we were teaching
and, as was his custom when we moved to a new
home, my husband asked the Lord for the protection
of four angels, one at each corner." Tom and Alison
held regular Bible studies at their home in English.
Most of those who came spoke English and when
someone came who did not they used an interpreter.
One Chinese lady said she could see angels in their
sitting room. Through an interpreter she said, "There
are four angels here. They come in to listen when
you talk about the Bible." Having confirmation of the
Lord's protection of their home was a great encouragement to Tom and Alison.

Protection of a more immediate sort was required
for Ruth Deakin and her family, when they were in
Ghana in 1983. It was a time of political unrest, eco-
nomic collapse, famine and drought. There was a
cholera epidemic at the hospital where her husband
worked, their house had been cursed by black magic
spells and, as the last straw, a cobra was stealing the

much-needed eggs from their hens. Ruth says, "I was beginning to feel overwhelmed by these circumstances until one night I had an experience where three people came into the bungalow. Two of them were angels and one was, I think, Christ Himself. They were all very tall and looked exceptionally strong. They were dressed in robes, rather than in modern clothing. The one who appeared to be Jesus took the two angels all around the bungalow, pointing out all the occupants, our two children, a nurse who was staying with us at the time, and ourselves. I had the impression He knew every detail about us. At the end of the tour, He turned to the two angels and said, 'On no account must anything happen to them because they are precious', and then the visitation finished. I subsequently felt a real sense of peace and faith that God was looking after our family, as did the rest of the household when I told them. It was not a dream, nor a hallucination, but a spiritual reality." The Deakin family did not know at the time that friends in Bristol, while praying for them, had specifically asked God to send angels to protect them.

A missionary who was alone and in dire need of help was Ginny Hales who, at the time (1967), was in her first year of teaching in Kenya. She writes, "It had been raining heavily and I was driving my little VW Beetle. Suddenly the thick mud caused the car to slither sideways until the back became firmly embedded in the ditch. I was so well stuck in the mud that only a forklift truck could have got me out. I tried to push it clear, but all in vain, so I got back into the car and locked myself in! I was in an area where bands of young thugs were terrorizing people and in Africa there is always danger from wild animals. For an hour, not a single vehicle passed, so I became in-

creasingly cold and scared. From time to time I tried
to get the car to move, to no avail, and all the time
I was praying with my whole heart for the Lord to
help me. As darkness fell, I suddenly had a strong
urge to start the engine again and, as I turned the key,
I felt the car move effortlessly out of the solid mud
of the ditch and back up on to the crest of the road!
The car was not yet in gear, and I was absolutely
dumbfounded! It felt just as if someone very strong
had pushed me out, but I looked around and not a
soul was in sight. I hadn't the slightest doubt that
God's angels were there. Some answers to prayer just
knock the breath out of you and this was one of
them." Ginny adds, "I bet if more missionaries were
aware of the book you are writing, you would never
come out from under the pile of their accounts!"

In various parts of the world there seem to have
been an unusual number of angel sightings. Medju-
gorje in Bosnia has for several years been a place
where many people have seen angels and also the
Virgin Mary in the sky. Italy has had many reported
sightings of angels, especially St. Michael, who is
said to have made one particular mountain his own.
This is now known as Monte Sant'Angelo and many
pilgrims visit the site. Also in Italy, Padre Pio, a
much-respected priest, was repeatedly visited by an
angel throughout his life, giving him special knowledge and insight, which enabled him to help others.
Zimbabwe in Africa suffered civil war for several
years during which there were many accounts of miraculous rescue and deliverance, due to God's intervention. Some of these involved angels giving
protection who appeared as "white soldiers" or
"white guards." Usually these were seen only by attackers who retreated. The people being protected did

not see the angels and only heard about them when
the raiders were captured and questioned later. This
kind of protection has happened to many missionaries
in various countries throughout the world, where
their message was being opposed.

The Reverend John Knight told me of an incident
which happened to him during those troubled years in
Zimbabwe. An international Christian leader had
come to speak in various places around the country
and John went to collect him from Harare to drive
him to speak at his church in Mutare. One stretch of
the road was particularly noted for ambushes on motorists so drivers were advised not to use it after
4 P.M. As they reached the village before this area at
5:30 P.M., John offered to stop there for the night and
resume their journey in the morning. The visitor,
however, was keen to carry on, so they did. On the
way the visitor silently repented to God for putting
both their lives at risk, and he felt the Lord tell him
that John's car was protected. Still silently, he asked
the Lord how John was being protected and was told
to look out of the window and upward. Above the car
he was shown the most enormous angel spread out
over the car with a flaming sword stretched out
ahead. This, he was told, was how John was always
protected. Surprisingly, he did not tell John about this
revelation, but later, on his return to Harare, he related it to a group of Christians, many of whom later
talked about it to John. The protection was apparently
ongoing as, during his many journeys, he had several
near misses but no injuries during those years of civil
war.

There have also been a number of accounts of lone
missionaries being saved from a mob of attackers.
Just as the situation seemed desperate, the crowd

slunk away, or rushed off terrified. In each case the missionary being rescued did not see how the release was achieved, and was amazed to be unharmed. Most of these accounts continue with a report that, some time later, one of the attackers met the person again, or had a change of heart, and explained that the missionary had suddenly been surrounded by a number of strong-looking "white guards." Usually it later transpires that the missionary was being prayed for back home at precisely the hour the attack was foiled, and the same number of people were praying as the number of guards who were seen.

On September 7, 1992, in Tansen, Nepal, amazing sights were witnessed in the sky. At least two people saw a large bright light, which they took to be an angel, descend rapidly from the sky and fly in the direction of the local church. The same evening, over a hundred others saw a vision in the sky of a man wearing a loin cloth, with arms outstretched and head bowed, attached to a large cross. This stayed in the sky for over an hour and many people were very moved by it. Most of those who saw the bright light and the cross are not Christians, so it has made them ask the believers many questions about God and Jesus. It has been a remarkable and thrilling experience for everyone who saw or has heard about these sightings.

On a more personal note, two children saw angels just before they died, which made a great impact on them. Roy Dodman is originally from Yorkshire, but is now a minister in Kingston, Jamaica. During a class he was teaching on evangelism, the subject arose about sharing the Christian faith with children. A nurse in the class told them of an experience which had been fixed firmly in her memory. She was nursing an eleven-year-old boy who had cancer in his leg. No one ever visited him and he seemed all alone in the world. The nurse shared very honestly with the class how she had struggled to know what to say to the lad, and how she had given him the twenty-third psalm to read, "The Lord is my shepherd."

The nurse suggested the boy replace the words "I, me and my" through the psalm with his own name, to make God's promises of security more personal for him. The nurse reports, "While I was changing the dressing on his leg, I told him that Jesus loved him and would be with him always, even if he became more ill. I frankly did not know what else to say, as I did not want to tell him bluntly that he was going to die. I started to clear up the trolley when the boy said, 'Do you see them, nurse?' I said, 'See who?' and looked out of the window, thinking he was watching someone outside. He asked, 'Can't you see the two angels standing in the room behind you?' He pointed to where they were, but I had to admit I couldn't see them, even though I believe angels come to help us. He told me that he wasn't afraid anymore of dying, because he knew Jesus loved him and he felt safe with the angels. After that, the other nurses noticed how much happier he was and wondered why. I told them about the angels, and the nurses felt the boy's ability to see the angels just then was a special gift from God. I had not needed to see the angels; they were especially for him. The boy died peacefully that night.

The other lad who saw angels was seventeen-year-old Jason Stroop, who was dying of leukemia at his home in St. Clair, Missouri. On May 13, 1992, Jason's brother, Scott, arrived home from Bible College to see Jason because he was so ill. As

Scott walked into the room, Jason asked him, "Who are the four friends with you?" Scott was alone, but Jason insisted, "What are their names? I wish I had a camera to take their photos, because they are so special. There is a beautiful, bright light around them." A little later Jason said "I've had enough pain. I want to go home. He slept peacefully then and, after time with the family, he died the following evening. Jason was a lovely lad, strong in faith, and his family was thankful for this special final gift he received.

Two English friends, Helen Mekie and Grace Longmire, have had adventures in several different countries where they have traveled to share the good news of Jesus. Usually just the two of them travel together, sometimes in very isolated places. There have been several occasions when they have been in potentially dangerous situations and have known God's protection in rescuing them. A few years ago they were driving through desert country in central Asia. They came upon a petrol pump, miles from anywhere, and needed to buy petrol as it was always many miles between pumps. There was a solitary man who looked at them villainously as if his intentions were anything but honorable. When they asked for petrol he demanded an extortionate amount of money in addition to the cost of the petrol. They refused to pay and he became very nasty. Just then, a soldier appeared from nowhere and pointed a gun at the pump attendant. He meekly filled the tank with petrol and accepted the correct amount of money. As he went to put the money in his box, Helen and Grace turned to thank the soldier, but he had disappeared. The land was flat for miles around, with no vegetation or buildings. There was nowhere he could

possibly have appeared from or disappeared to. They
both knew at once that he was an angel sent by God
to rescue them.

On another occasion, when driving toward Afghan-
istan, as they turned a corner, Helen and Grace saw
that a tree-trunk had been deliberately placed across
the road, so they had to stop. They were immediately
surrounded by a band of more than a hundred Arab
men. As Helen and Grace refused to get out of
the car, the men gathered around and lifted the vehicle up. It was very frightening. Helen asked, "What
shall we do?" Grace replied, "Pray to the Lord in
tongues." Immediately they started to pray they were
surrounded by a cloud of dust. The men backed off,
looking terrified. As they retreated they quickly
moved the tree-trunk and said desperately, "Please
leave at once." Grace and Helen were only too glad
to do so. As they drove safely away, they were certain that the band of men had seen an army of angels,
stronger and greater in number than the bandits.
Helen and Grace had seen only the cloud of dust as
they had not needed to see the angels, but they
praised God for this miraculous escape.

Helen and Grace had a further experience of angelic help when they were in an uncomfortable rather
than life-threatening situation. They were in Turkey
and traveling to Greece by road and ferry. Before
leaving the campsite where they spent the night, they
had filled up their water bottles from the tap marked
"drinking water" ready for the long, hot journey.
However, when they stopped for a drink, they found
it was salty water and they could not drink it. With
their remaining Turkish money they bought some or-
ange juice but then could buy no more drinks until
they got into Greece and could use their Greek

money. It was a very hot day, so by the time they
were sitting in their car in the line for the ferry, they
were feeling very thirsty indeed. Grace suddenly said,
"It would be lovely to have some watermelon to
quench our thirst." Helen told her it was most un-
helpful to make them think of such a thing as there
was no earthly possibility of getting any. At that moment, Helen was tapped on the shoulder through the
open window and a large slice of watermelon was
passed to her. As she handed it across to Grace, another piece was passed into the car. No money was
asked for and whoever brought it had disappeared.
Dumbfounded, Helen asked, "Where did that come
from?" Grace answered, "Well, I did ask the Lord for
some." The man waiting in the car behind them, seeing this, went to find out if he could buy some watermelon, but came back after several minutes saying he
could not find anyone anywhere who had any watermelon. He had been unable to find the man whom he
had watched give some to Helen and Grace, which
they had by now consumed with delight!

I have also been given a fascinating book about the
remarkable protection afforded many times to a Nor-
wegian missionary, Marie Monsen, in China during
the 1920s. As the book is now out of print, it seems
right to share one of the accounts it contains. At that
time lawlessness was rife in China, with hordes of
brigands attacking innocent people on the roads and
in their homes. Even the Chinese army was not beyond reproach. One night the leader of the soldiers
promised them that they could loot a city one night as
he had been unable to pay them for so long. This city
housed the headquarters of the mission for which
Marie worked, and she was there that night. Rumors

had been heard that the looting would start at 10 P.M., but the soldiers were impatient and began at 8 P.M.

Marie and the Chinese Christians with her heard shooting and shouting all night, but no soldier came to bang on the door of their compound. However, all through the night, terrified neighbors kept arriving to take refuge with them. They climbed into the compound over the walls, each carrying a little bundle of valuables in case their homes were burnt to the ground by the soldiers. There were many fires to be seen around the city and much commotion everywhere. All night Marie and the Chinese Christians with her welcomed the fearful neighbors, made them comfortable and shared with them the peace that only God can give. The non-believing neighbors saw the difference a Christian faith made to these people, who had no fear of the city-wide attack happening all around, which could have invaded their own compound at any moment. As the bullets whistled overhead, Marie shared with all of them the comfort in the words of Psalm 91:5: "You will not fear the terror of the night, nor the arrow that flies by day," in her own words substituting bullets for arrows.

The following morning, many of the other people who lived near the compound came to ask who their "protectors" were. At first Marie was not sure what they meant, until she heard the same account from so many people that she knew it was true. They all separately said they had seen three tall foreign (not Chinese) soldiers standing on the high roof of their Gospel Hall, one at each end and one in the middle. A fourth protector was sitting on the porch over the main gate, keeping watch in every direction. They were there all night, and all the accounts said they "shone." Neither Marie nor any of her Christian friends had seen them. Only the non-believers living nearby had seen these angel protectors, to convince them that God takes care of all who trust in Him.

# CHAPTER FIFTEEN

# *The Church's View*

**K**arl Barth, a renowned Swiss Protestant theologian of this century said, "The Church still tells us, in ever so many ways, that angels are not to be doubted or denied." Throughout history the Church has included an understanding of the ministry of angels among its beliefs. However, although many denominations assume their existence and ability to intervene in our lives, they rarely specifically teach about angels.

Early and medieval theology evolved a complex speculative arrangement of the angelic world. Pseudo-Dionysius, who lived in the fifth century, described separate entities of angels and grouped them in three hierarchies, each including three categories: the highest, seraphim, cherubim and thrones; in the middle dominions, powers and authorities; and finally, principalities, archangels and angels. The basis of these groupings is said to be Colossians 1:16 and Ephesians 1:21, where these titles are mentioned but not explained. The exact dates of Pseudo-Dionysius

193

are not known, nor even his real name, as he chose to
write under the pseudonym of Dionysius the Areopa-
gite, a first-century convert of St. Paul in Athens
(Acts 17:34). However, the influence of this enig-
matic figure is clearly seen on spiritual writers from
the early Middle Ages onward.

Thomas Aquinas, an Italian theologian of the thirteenth century, known as the Angelic Doctor, adopted
a similar scheme to the angelic hierarchy of Pseudo-
Dionysius. He discussed and wrote about it fully, but
was more interested in the nature of angels as individual spiritual substances occupying space. His writings were extensive, the most influential of his works
being *Summa Theologica,* a systematic presentation
of Christian doctrine. This was adopted as the official
teaching of the Roman Catholic Church by Leo XIII
(Pope from 795 to 816 AD). During the Middle Ages,
angels were widely believed in and accepted. For example, many English farmers in the thirteenth century would have found it easier to believe that angels
visited England than in the existence of other farmers
in France!

The reformer Martin Luther (1483–1546) was a
well-educated monk and priest. He became a renowned doctor of theology, while at the same time
wrestling with doubt over his personal salvation, despite numerous arduous penances. His studies of
Scripture led him to realize that we are saved "by
grace alone" through faith in Jesus, not by our own
deserving. On the subject of dying, Luther said we
will "only rest in God, just as we sleep sweetly in
this life, under the protection of God and the angels,
fearing no danger even though surrounded by devils."
On another occasion he said, "One angel is more
powerful than all the devils put together."

The Council of Trent, which met in three stages from 1545 to 1563 decided that angels intercede for men and that "it is good and profitable to invoke them suppliantly ... for the purpose of obtaining benefits from God through His Son Jesus Christ." John Calvin (1509–64), a French reformer, who preached widely during his lifetime, wrote:

*With regard to angels ... the care and protection of the pious has been committed to them. They must therefore, in obedience to God, be solicitous about our salvation, and they only discharge the duty assigned them by praying for us. God declares that all the angels watch over the protection of the righteous.*

Calvin saw that the error in so much teaching on angels was the complicated speculation which had built up over the centuries and which bore scant resemblance to Biblical teaching. For example, the Bible specifically says in Colossians 2:18 and Revelation 22:9 that we should not worship angels, or pray to or through them. Christians have the privilege to speak to God directly, because Jesus has removed the barrier of sin by His death and resurrection.

On September 29 each year, St. Michael and All Angels are remembered in the Church's calendar, both Anglican and Roman Catholic. On that day the Anglican Collect states:

*Eternal Lord God, who ordained and constituted the service of angels and men in a wonderful order: grant that as Your holy angels always serve You in heaven, so by Your appoint-*

*ment they may help and defend us on earth;
through Jesus Christ our Lord. Amen.*

The Bible readings, hymns and sermon for this day
especially point us to the ministry of angels. While
singing hymns the references to angels can wash over
us, as if they are just words, without our realizing the
significance of these magnificent beings:

*Angels and archangels may have gathered
    there,
Cherubim and seraphim thronged the air.*
                            CHRISTINA ROSSETTI

*Heaven's arches rang when the angels sang.*
                            EMILY ELLIOTT

*Angels in bright raiment rolled the stone away.*
                            E. L. BUDRY

*Angels, from the realms of glory,
Wing your flight o'er all the earth;
Ye who sang creation's story,
Now proclaim Messiah's birth.*

                            J. MONTGOMERY

*Angel voices ever singing round Thy throne of
    light.*

                            FRANCIS POTT

*Ye holy angels bright,
Who wait at God's right hand,
Or through the realms of light
Fly at your Lord's command.*

                            RICHARD BAXTER

*Come let us join our cheerful songs*
*With angels round the throne;*
*Ten thousand thousand are their tongues*
*But all their joy are one.*

ISAAC WATTS

*Hark! the herald angels sing*
*"Glory to the newborn King"*

CHARLES WESLEY

The Roman Catholic Church teaches about angels more frequently than the other denominations. The General Secretary of the Catholic Bishops' Conference of England and Wales wrote to me saying that: "The Church believes in the existence of angels and has quite a lot to say about their nature and role." *Angels—Spirits Magnificent and Mighty* by Athanasius Recheis, a Catholic monk, stated in 1976: "The Bible portrays angels in a two-fold function: (a) they stand before God singing His praises and (b) they are sent into the world, especially to certain individuals, as messengers and executors of God's decrees (Hebrews 1:14)." He also wrote: "The believing Christian will even today maintain that there are angels because the Bible and the Church teach it."

The official Roman Catholic view was declared at the 4th Lateran Council (1215) and reaffirmed at the 1st Vatican Council (1870): "We firmly believe ... that God is the sole source of all things visible and invisible, things spiritual and material. By His Almighty power, in the beginning of time, He created in like manner both orders of creation out of nothing, the spiritual and the material, that is the world of angels and the physical world." The feast day on September 29 in the Roman Catholic Church has developed into the veneration of specific angels so is now called the day for "Saints Michael, Gabriel and Raphael, Archangels." The Bible calls Michael an archangel, and says he is "one of the chief princes" and "the great Prince." Gabriel, however, is called an angel, as is Raphael, but the latter only in the Apocrypha. These Jewish writings were not included in the Bible as they do not bear the same stamp of authority as the Old and New Testaments. Another archangel, Jeremiel, and another angel, Uriel, are also mentioned in the Apocrypha, but they are hardly ever heard about today. Gabriel and Raphael both describe themselves as "standing in the presence of the Lord" (Luke 1:19 and Tobit 12:15).

The Christian Bible consists of the Hebrew Scripture of the Jews and the New Testament, which is a collection of books written about Jesus and the meaning of life, death and resurrection to eternal life. The collection which makes up the Christian Bible was added to during several centuries and was finally agreed at a council in Carthage in 397 AD. At the time of the Reformation, the Protestant Church regarded the Apocrypha as edifying reading, as the Anglican lectionary puts it, "for example of life, but not to establish any doctrine"; while the Roman Catholic Church included the Apocryphal writings as part of the Old Testament. What makes the books of the Bible different from all other books is that they have been inspired by God, speaking through its human authors, giving it His own true authority.

The Protestant view on angels is summed up by Professor Louis Berkhof in his *Systematic Theology,* first published in 1941:

*There are clear evidences of belief in the existence of angels from the very beginning of the Christian era. Some of them were regarded as good, and others as evil. The former were held in high esteem as personal beings of a lofty order, endowed with moral freedom engaged in the joyful service of God, and employed by God to minister to the welfare of men. In distinction from God, angels are created beings . . . as creatures, they are finite and limited, though they stand in a freer relationship to time and space than man . . . They are personal beings endowed with intelligence and will . . . While not omniscient, they are superior in knowledge to men . . . They always behold the face of God, are our exemplars in doing the will of God and possess eternal life . . . It is perfectly safe to say that the angels constitute an innumerable company, a mighty host. Their full number was created in the beginning; there has been no increase. Their ordinary service consists first of all in their praising God day and night. The extraordinary service of the angels was made necessary by the fall of man, and forms an important element in the special revelation of God. They often mediate the revelations of God, communicate blessings to His people, and execute judgment upon His enemies.*

My husband, Geoff, as an Anglican vicar, has helped me in the research for this chapter. This has included writing to all the major Christian denominations in Great Britain. Some have responded most helpfully and positively on the subject.

The Free Church of Scotland sent the transcript of

a lecture delivered by the Reverend Professor James Fraser at the opening of the Free Church College in October 1982. He encapsulated the angelic beliefs of the Free Church, giving a clear overview of the subject of angels, including the following: "As the untiring servants of Jehovan [another name for God] the ministry of the angels is continual and varied. Whatever the Lord's bidding is, they fulfil it promptly and efficiently. They are His servants, not that the infinite Jehovah requires attendants. Whatever they do, they do it to the LORD. But the gracious ministry of angels on behalf of the people of God is not insignificant or infrequent. Though angels' visits may be 'few and far between' their service is not confined to their appearances. I believe that there is an ongoing ministry of angels to the Church of which we are mainly unaware. The interest in angels and their ministry is a healthy one if kept within the bounds of Scripture; a Biblical assessment is proper and edifying. To neglect the angels altogether is to leave ourselves ignorant of an important part of Scriptural revelation concerning a vast army of glorious beings with whom we shall share eternity, and to whom we are, even now, indebted as those who minister, by God's command, for the heirs of salvation."

The Reverend Wynne Lewis, the General Superintendent of the Elim Pentecostal Church, replied to the request with, "As a denomination, we do not have a doctrinal view on angels today although, in our churches, we certainly believe in angelic visitations and ministration. We believe that they are servants of the Most High, sent to minister to God's children on earth. There are several instances of their preserving powers in alarming situations. We are experiencing their assistance in so many ways."

The official view of the Salvation Army was sent to me by their Editor-in-Chief, Lieutenant Colonel Maxwell Ryan, who wrote: "Salvationists generally hold a Biblical view of angels and their activities in the world today. Along with other Christians, Salvationists believe that angels are heavenly beings who have been created by God to do His bidding. They hold the view that there are also fallen angels who work against God and humanity, by seeking to do the will of Satan, who is their master. Salvationists hold that the angels who remained loyal to God are not intermediaries between God and humanity—that position is held by Jesus Christ, who is 'far superior to the angels' (Hebrews 1:4)—but are 'ministering spirits' (Hebrews 1:14). The ministry of angels to people may take various forms, as is indicated by the Biblical record of their interaction with humanity."

Basil Varnam, the General Administrator of the Assemblies of God, replied, "I must advise that we have issued no official doctrinal papers on our position toward angels. However, I have no doubt that, if asked, the general view of our ministers and congregations would be that they believe firmly in the ministry of angels today, because they are in the Bible. Hebrews 1 particularly comes to mind. We do, from time to time, hear of instances in the twentieth century where angels have been seen. Sincere Christians have testified to the intervention of these heavenly beings, often at times of crisis, and we rejoice to hear of God responding to the needs of His people through the ministration of angels."

In the early days of the Missions to Seamen, the wife and sister of one of the chaplains, the Reverend William Kingston, were jointly responsible for choosing the emblem of the Missions. They made a flag on

February 27, 1858, which included a flying angel based on Revelation 14:6: "I saw an angel flying in mid-air, and he had the eternal gospel to proclaim to those who live on the earth—to every nation, tribe, language and people."

Mother Alexandra, who is the Abbess of the Orthodox Monastery of the Transfiguration in Ellwood City, Pennsylvania, wrote a book in 1987 called *The Holy Angels.*

*It was early morning when I was seven years old, that I saw the Angels. I am as sure of it now as I was then. I was not dreaming nor seeing things. I just know they were there, plainly, clearly, distinctly. I was neither astonished nor afraid. I was not even awed—I was only terribly pleased. I wanted to talk to them and touch them. The Angels have a stupendous reality. Their activity among us has become to me a vital, positive reality.*

This Orthodox nun was born in 1909 in Bucharest, Romania, youngest daughter of King Ferdinand and Queen Marie. She is described as "a beautiful woman of regal dignity."

The New Churches' Network and the Apostolic Churches hold an evangelical and Biblical view of angels. Gerald Coates is Director of Pioneer, which is "dedicated to promoting dynamic and effective Christianity." Gerald said, "Our only doctrinal view of angels is that they played a prominent part in the Old Testament, and a very significant part in Jesus's ministry—therefore we still believe they are active today. Our understanding is, quite simply, that there are angels operating today in the same way that they were throughout the Old and New Testament and therefore we should expect them to operate today. In the West as a whole, our level of faith is very low and our spiritual perceptions dull. But we, personally, believe in the role of angels today."

Basilea Schlink, author of many books, is founder of the worldwide Evangelical Sisterhood of Mary, in Darmstadt, Germany. The following extract from her book *The Unseen World of Angels and Demons* is used with her permission.

*The angels of God are bright and shining beings, emanating light and mirroring the glory of God. Often when angels appear visibly, people fall to the ground, overwhelmed by their radiance, grandeur and power. In the angels they encounter something of God's holiness. Everything about them magnifies the beauty, glory, majesty and omnipotence of God. Today we have forgotten what an elevated position the angels have before God. We no longer treat the angels with respect, nor do we have a wholesome fear of demons. Both attitudes expose us more to the attacks of demons and cause us much harm and suffering. What a source of strength it would be for us to know that the holy armies of heaven, the angels, are battling on behalf of us weak mortals!*

The Baptist denomination is a union of independent churches. As such, there is only a basic declaration of principle held jointly, but all Baptists believe in the teaching of the Bible. This view transcends denominational boundaries, uniting those who believe and proclaim the good news of Jesus Christ. Angels

are believed in and accepted for the part they play in
the whole Bible, and for their relevance today. One of
the most well-known Baptists in America is Dr. Billy
Graham, the worldwide evangelist. He has written
several booklets about angels, as well as the inform-
ative book *Angels—God's Secret Agents,* published in
1975.

The official bodies of the United Reformed
Church, the Methodist Church and the Religious Society of Friends (Quakers) all replied that not much
thought was given to angels at an official level. However, I have received accounts of angel experiences
from members of all three denominations.

Overall, the Church's view of angels is derived
from the Bible's teaching of their closeness to God
and their value in helping us. It is the Holy Spirit
who reveals to us our need of Jesus and His deep
love for us. The angels' faithful service is based on
their love for God so their ministry to us is a response to God's wishes.

# CHAPTER SIXTEEN

# *Conclusion*

A poem from *Wild Goose,* an anthology
from Iona, the Christian community off the
west coast of Scotland, includes the words:

*Give us a message ... send us an angel*
*that will start us seeking a new way of life.*

If a scientist is asked, "What is electricity?", he
will probably say that it is a form of energy. It may
be perceived as heat, light, power or a shock. But, in
itself, it is none of these things. They are merely out-
ward manifestations of an invisible force of energy.
When an angel appears to a person, it is in a form he
can recognize, as a courtesy, but what angels are in
themselves is far greater than this visible manifesta-
tion.

We shall all see angels at some time in our lives,
at the Judgment Day, if not before. "The harvest is
the end of the age, and the harvesters are the angels"
(Matthew 13:39). Those who have seen angels in this
life are fortunate, because they have seen evidence

that God is active in the world today. Most of us have not yet seen an angel, since it has not been in God's plan for us, but it has nothing to do with our level of faith, devotion or understanding. Philipa Dodd of Solihull wrote, "Whatever doubts I had as a girl, whatever doubts I sometimes have now, I know there is a God, and I know I saw the angels take my dad to heaven."

My own son, Luke, has had two experiences of seeing angels and is the only person in our family who has. The first was when I was putting him to bed at the age of eleven weeks. My husband and I had just prayed for his safety for the night, as we always did, since I was concerned about the danger of "crib death." As I was tucking him in and talking to him, Luke, as usual, was gurgling and chuckling happily at me. Then his gaze was taken upward and backward until he was looking at the blank wall behind him. The remarkable thing was that he was responding in exactly the same way to the wall as he just had been to me. At that age babies only respond to smiling faces, bright colors and music, and Luke was chuckling and gurgling as if he saw a smiling face. Mystified by his response, I looked to where his gaze fell and I saw a brilliant-white, head-and-shoulders shape on the wall. I did not see a face, as Luke must have, but the room was filled with an incredible, tangible sense of peace. I delightedly told my husband about it, and wrote the details in Luke's baby-book.

When Luke was seven, he came down to breakfast on the morning of March 30, 1982. He said, "Some men came to visit me in the night." Luke had been having lots of bad dreams recently so, thinking he must have been dreaming again, we asked what they were like. "They were taller than Daddy [who is nearly six foot] and they wore white, well a sort of bluish-white," he replied. "They had very kind faces and one of them spoke to me; he said I will only have happy dreams now, and I will have a good life and he will come back when I am nineteen." We said, "You must have been dreaming", but Luke was adamant that he was awake when these four or five men came to see him. He said he was not at all frightened but was glad they came. I don't think we had ever told Luke about his previous angel experience until that point. It certainly wasn't a subject we discussed much at home, so there is no reason why he should have made up this experience. He was always truthful and he was normally readily able to distinguish between being awake or not. We then told him about his experience as a baby and we all believed this present experience was also angels.

Many people have heard the story of the hitch-hiker who, after having been picked up at the roadside, engages the driver in conversation. During the journey, he raises the subject of Jesus and his final comment is "Jesus is coming back soon." With that, he disappears from the moving car, without the door having been opened. Inevitably the driver is astounded at the sudden disappearance of his passenger. In some cases, he has pulled over to the side of the road, to think through what has just happened. Sometimes a policeman has stopped to ask if there is any problem. The driver, explaining about the disappearing hitch-hiker, is amazed to hear that the same policeman has heard of several identical incidents in that area. I have heard of this happening not only in different parts of Great Britain, but also in America and Australia. Perhaps Someone is trying to tell us something!

Nobody knows how many times an angel has stepped in, unseen, to protect us. Since most of us have never seen an angel, it is impossible to say how many times they have prevented a tragedy, but we can recognize the results of their care. "He will command His angels concerning you, to guard you in all your ways; they will lift you up in their hands, so that you will not strike your foot against a stone . . . 'Because he loves me,' says the Lord, 'I will rescue him; I will protect him, for he acknowledges My name' " (Psalm 91:11–14).

After Roberta Bowman of Halesowen saw cherubs, she said, "It was an electrifying experience. I *never* thought cherubs were real, just things you saw on Christmas cards; but they are very real and the awesome presence of God filled the place." When Val West of Ringwood wrote about having seen angels she said, "It is only a small experience, but tremendous for me; it has done me a power of good, remembering it and setting it down on paper." Pamela Smith of Shoreham said, "I had an angel experience when I was seven and I am now sixty-eight, but it is as clear in my mind as if it were yesterday. I had gone to bed and it was dark. Suddenly my room was filled with very bright light and there appeared at the window a beautiful face with white feathered wings. She looked at me and I was filled with joy. Then she was gone and darkness returned. I felt no fear and did not even call my mother, but went off to sleep feeling very happy. All my life I have regarded this as a sign that God's angels are guarding us."

Mary-Rose Atkins's sight of an angel was also as a face at the window. At the age of eighteen, life was extremely fraught for her, as she was caring for her ill father, who was often obstreperous and difficult.

One night she lay in bed feeling very stressed and could not sleep. Mary-Rose says, "Suddenly I saw a face at the window looking at me. I am 100 percent certain he was an angel. He looked like a cherub, surrounded by a beautiful light and his wings glistened. His face shone with a beautiful look of concern. I did not feel frightened as I gazed on his face, but a great sense of peace descended on me and I breathed, 'Thank you, God.' I am now forty-four and remember the angel like it was yesterday."

Something very similar happened to Beryl Jones on June 22, 1955. She had given birth that morning to her first child, a pretty dark-haired boy weighing 4 pounds 11 ounces. A friend of Beryl's who was a nurse at the same hospital had been allowed to see him in the premature baby unit and called in at 10.30 P.M. with the encouraging news that his previous blue coloring had now become a healthy pink. She also told Beryl that the sister on the premature baby unit could not understand why he had received emergency baptism that afternoon because, in her professional opinion, Philip was a good weight and was going to be fine. "My friend told me," says Beryl, "that there was no need whatsoever to be anxious for him, and that I should go to sleep, knowing all was well."

Beryl was really encouraged by this, and lay back on her pillows to rest. She continues, "In a little while, I became aware that someone was watching me. I turned toward the window and there, looking in from the outside, stood a nurse. I was so pleased to see her and, as the window was open, I asked her to come in to talk to me. Then I corrected myself saying, "No, come in and fetch me," to which she responded with a smile, that I understood to mean she had not come for me. With that, she turned her head

and left. I looked at my watch and it was ten past
eleven, exactly twelve hours since my son was born.
In about ten minutes, the doctor came into my room
and said to me, 'I'm very sorry, Mrs. Jones . . .' Before he could say any more, I completed the sentence
for him saying, 'My baby died at ten past eleven.'
The doctor was amazed that I knew. He asked if he
could fetch anyone for me or do anything. All I asked
was that he should close the window."

Beryl was new to the town and had not stayed in
the hospital before, so, seeing the nurse outside the
window, she assumed she was in a ground-floor
room. When she was well enough to get out of bed,
she looked out of the window and found she was on
the third floor. The person outside the window could
not have been a nurse, although Beryl spoke to her
and she responded. How could Beryl have known,
from so little communication, that baby Philip had
died? She was not told until the doctor walked into
her room. Yet later, in her bereavement, she was
comforted by remembering that the angel had minis-
tered to her in her hour of need. In those days, the
husband had to say goodbye to his wife at reception,
when she was admitted to give birth. Beryl's husband
had quoted to her there, "When you pass through the
waters, I will be with you . . . for I am the Lord"
(Isaiah 43:2). At the time, she had thought it a
strange verse to quote, since she was there for the
joyful purpose of giving birth to her first, much-
wanted baby. But, in the event, she was thankful that
she had been reminded of that verse, because God
sent His angel to visit her when she was "passing
through the waters," which in her case meant bereavement.

Shan Palmes wrote to me about two connected experiences she had several years ago. Unusually for her, she found herself wide awake one night, although it was very dark in the room. Suddenly an angel came from the direction of the door to stand beside her bed. She says, "He was about eight feet tall and I knew at once it was an angel, because of the extraordinary brightness around the whole figure, looking so pure. Perhaps the light was something like burning magnesium, because it would make the brightest electric light look a dowdy yellow by comparison, yet it didn't hurt the eyes. I could see the beautiful face clearly and thought it similar to a young man in the prime of life. He had dark clusters of curls framing his face, there were huge folded wings and the body was just brightness. He stood beside me for a few minutes, saying nothing; I was so surprised and amazed that I said nothing either, and then I suddenly realized that he had gone.

"Then I was seeing a distant picture, where the wall should have been. It was nighttime and I was looking down on our house, which had an angel kneeling above the roof, with wings folded and hands clasped in prayer. The picture faded as if a thin veil was pulled across my sight and I was back in my bedroom, sitting bolt upright! As I lay down thinking about this lovely experience, I felt very comforted by the revelation, realizing I was being guarded by angels. I was going through a very difficult time during this period of my life, with a lot of opposition to my faith in God; the knowledge that God's angels were protecting me was a tremendous help."

This protective help was required only three days later, as Shan explains: "March 1 was a dark, wet morning when I dropped off my third child at school. My youngest son, aged two, was strapped in his car-

seat attached to the front bench seat of our
Dormobile. As we set off on our homeward journey,
I was singing while my son added the Alleluias and
clapped his hands! As I pulled out from the school
entrance, a dark blue car hurtled around the corner,
traveling very fast. As I had reached about the middle
of the road, it hit us on the driver's side, and tipped
the Dormobile over sideways. Seconds later, the
'stranger to the area' driver of the dark blue car came
to me, white as a sheet, saying in awe: 'I can't understand it. The Dormobile went almost completely over
on its side and then to my amazement, came back up
again! Your son should certainly have been killed.' I
heard his words and knew instantly that it must have
been an angel who rescued us and prevented a terrible accident. I understood why I had been allowed to
see an angel three nights previously, although I had
never really given much thought to angels before. I
praise God that He sends His angels to watch over us
and is 'an ever-present help in trouble' (Psalm 46:1)."

Shan's experience of having a vision of an angel
over the roof of her house, while she was still in her
bedroom, reminded me of a similar incident which I
described in Chapter 1. There, an angel was seen giving protection to a home and family which would
otherwise have received a direct hit from a bomb the
same night.

It sometimes happens that angels are present in a
Christian gathering but appear in different forms to
different people. One evening at a New Wine 1992
meeting, in Shepton Mallet, Somerset, the subject
was "The healing power of God." Prue Bedwell saw
a ten-foot tall angel standing on the platform beside
David Pytches, the speaker. Prue described the angel
as brilliant, gleaming and powerful. At the same

time, Barry Kissell saw another angel standing on the platform next to the big screen used for overhead projection. The angel looked like a Roman soldier, wearing armor and holding a sword. He was life-sized, the height of an ordinary man, not as tall as the one Prue saw. Robin Lapwood's eyes were closed but he also sensed that a tall angel was standing on the platform. Prue, Barry and Robin were all sitting in the front row, just in front of the platform.

George Bennett was the warden at Crowhurst, a center for Christian healing in Sussex. One night he was called to see a woman who was apparently dying. He spent some time quietly holding her hand and praying for her. By the morning, however, she had recovered and later was able to go home. Her husband was the commander of a naval base, so, following her unexpected recovery, she immediately formed prayer fellowship groups throughout the naval base which many people were glad to attend. Some time later George was invited to a dinner party at their home. During the course of the dinner, she said to him, "Wasn't it wonderful how that night the whole room was filled with angels?" George replied, "Yes, I am glad you saw them too; I was conscious of them at the time." It was the first time either of them had mentioned the experience.

Sometimes several people can be involved in an answer to prayer, which is exciting when the various contributions are pieced together. This happened in October 1992 when Tom and Alison Donachie had been ministering to Gillian, who was being spiritually oppressed by evil forces. She had been feeling threatened and under attack when she was in her home. Tom and Alison, in praying for her, had asked Jesus to cleanse her home in Galashiels and for angels to protect her there. The atmosphere immediately changed to one of peace right through the house.

Meanwhile, a friend in Nottingham, Ted, who knew Gillian, was praying with his pastor, Alan, who was visiting him. Alan expressed concern that Gillian's son, who is unstable, might cause her harm by trying arson. Ted immediately replied, "It's OK, angels are protecting Gillian and her home—I've seen them." Ted knew nothing about Tom and Alison's specific prayer for angelic protection. At the same time, Philip, another friend, who is in Wakefield prison, but has become a Christian, was also praying for Gillian. He received a special word from the Lord that angels were guarding Gillian in her home. Jesus is not bound by time or place!

Alison Cross of Birmingham had two experiences in 1973 which changed her life. Her father was seriously ill in the hospital in Swindon, so she and her family visited him most weekends. The school where Alison taught had Wednesday, November 4, as a holiday so she traveled alone that day to Swindon to visit him. On entering the intensive care unit she was delighted to find him looking much better. Alison says, "My mother was sitting on the right-hand side of my father, but my eyes were drawn to the left side where I saw an angel in shining apparel. I knew the angel was warning me of my father's death and I could not bear to think I was going to lose him. My reaction was 'No' and I felt the angel respond, 'I will be back.' This must have all happened in a few seconds, as when I looked around me, everything was back to 'normal.'

"My father went into a coma on November 21," continues Alison, "but on Monday, December 3, as I left school, the angel seemed to be with me. Although I did not see it, I knew the angel was with me for the rest of the day; I could feel his presence all evening. My mother phoned at 7:15 A.M. the following morning to say my father had died at 1:30 A.M. so was at last released from his suffering. This 'angel of mercy' brought me a revelation that was the start of a new life in our Lord Jesus Christ. For myself it was a whole new beginning."

Angels are found in other faiths, particularly Judaism and Islam. Jews and Christians share the Old Testament as their Holy Bible, so our understanding of angels is the same. In Christianity, the Jews' longed-for Messiah has been found in Jesus, so our New Testament goes on to tell of His life and ministry and the way the Good News about Him spread throughout the then-known world. In Islam, the angels of the Old Testament are also accepted as being God's messengers, since part of the Koran is based on the Old Testament. In all traditions, angels are seen as worshiping God in heaven and being sent to earth to do specific tasks as He commands.

In the *Phaedrus* Plato said that the souls of men and "the gods" had wings. In Egyptian religion there were many winged animals, whose wings represented power and domination. The Sioux Indians speak of winged men, the shaman of Eastern Peru have good spirits appearing in human form. In Zoroastrianism, Taoism and Buddhism, rituals are performed to call down angels into statues or into the humans performing the rituals. New Age selects from many religions so includes spirits and angels as being part of the inner consciousness. These beliefs do not share the Christian understanding that God alone is in charge of angels and of all life. Only He is worthy of worship and Jesus is the only mediator between God

and man. There is no need to invoke any other mediator or spiritual being.

The Bible does not try to prove the existence of
angels, it just takes them for granted. In Old and New
Testament alike, it is clear that a certainty in the reality of God's angels is unquestioned. Their purpose
toward God is to do perfectly what we on earth do so
imperfectly, that is, to worship Him. Whenever the
Bible describes angels worshiping God it is always a
corporate activity—"a great multitude," "a mighty
host." Belief in angels can help to preserve us from
the dangers of superstition, the occult and communi-
cating with spirits.

If we are tempted to despair because of the power
of evil in the world today, then a belief in God's angels reminds us of the vast multitude on the side of
good, fighting in the battle against sin, the successful
outcome of which is already certain. We are never
alone in the battle. This was typified in what happened to the prophet Elisha in 2 Kings 6:15–17. Elisha's servant was horrified to see that they were
surrounded by an army of enemy horses and chariots.
He asked Elisha, "What are we to do?" Elisha replied, "Don't be afraid, those who are with us are
more than those who are with them," and he prayed,
"O Lord, open his eyes so that he may see." Then the
Lord opened the servant's eyes, and he looked and
saw the hills full of horses and chariots of fire all
around Elisha. In the spiritual battle, there are always
more angels on the side of God than evil spirits seeking to cause harm. If we are tempted to be fearful, the
thought of the presence of God's angels should sus-
tain us, although in their own strength they cannot
save, but only carry out God's will.

Part of my research into the subject has been at the

Alister Hardy Research Center in Oxford, which includes several hundred angel experiences. I have not included any of them in this book as they have not been sent to me directly by the people concerned. I would not, therefore, have been able to have further contact with them and verify their honesty, sanity and resulting effects of their experience.

It is not right to place too much emphasis on angels. Perhaps if we could keep angels in the right perspective, neither overemphasizing them, nor refusing to recognize their validity, we would be allowed to see them more often. Many people who have written to me have said they have been grateful for the opportunity to share their experience of angels which has invariably made a great difference in their life. Yet no matter how thrilling the impact of an angelic visit may be, we must keep our eyes on God's Son, Jesus; millions of angels put together have far less power and authority than the Lord Jesus.

# BIBLIOGRAPHY

All Bible references are from the New International Version. The titles that follow are listed in the order in which reference is made to them within the text.

## CHAPTER SIX
### *Cherub, Seraph and Archangel*

*New Catholic Encyclopedia*, Vol. 1, compiled by Catholic University of America, McGraw-Hill, 1967

*Angels, Cherubim and Gods*, Anon., Wertheim, Mackintosh and Hunt, 1861

## CHAPTER EIGHT
### *Angels in History*

*Butler's Lives of the Saints,* Burns & Oates, 1985

*The Holy Angels*, Rev. R. O'Kennedy, Burns & Oates, 1887

*Joan of Arc*, Marina Warner, Vintage, 1981

*Joan of Arc*, John Holland Smith, Sidgwick & Jackson, 1973

*Saint Joan of Arc*, Vita Sackville-West, Cobden-Sanderson, 1936

*William Blake*, Michael Davis, Paul Elek Ltd, 1977

*When He is Come*, Eifion Evans, Evangelical Movement of Wales, 1959

*Sadhu Sundar Singh*, Phyllis Thompson, Operation Mobilisation Publishing, 1992

*Phoenix at Coventry*, Basil Spence, Geoffrey Bles, 1962

# CHAPTER NINE
## Angels in World War I

*Illustrated London News*, September 12, 1914

*On the Side of the Angels*, Harold Begbie, Hodder & Stoughton, 1915

*Angels at Mons in the Light of Holy Scripture*, Bristol, 1916

*We Have a Guardian*, 4th edition, W. B. Grant, The Covenant Publishing Co., 1952

*The Church of England and the First World War*, Alan Wilkinson, S.P.C.K.

*1914 Glory Departing*, Edward Owen, Buchan & Enright Publishers

*Angels of Mons*, Credo, E. Austin & Son, 1960

*The Smoke & the Fire: Myths & Anti-myths of War 1861–1945*, John Terraine, Sidgwick & Jackson, 1980

*This England*, Winter 1982

*Essex Yeomanry Journal*, 1989

*The Great War . . . I was there: Undying memories of*

*1914–18,* ed. Sir John Hammerton, The London Amalgamated Press Ltd

# CHAPTER TEN
## Angels at Bedsides

*The Living Touch,* Dorothy Kerin, Burrswood, 1914

# CHAPTER THIRTEEN
## Angels and Men

*Thirst after God,* Denis Ball, Marshall Pickering, 1987

# CHAPTER FOURTEEN
## Angels Abroad

*Rain in a Dry Land,* John Knight, Hodder & Stoughton, 1987
*A Present Help,* Marie Monsen, China Inland Mission, 1960

# CHAPTER FIFTEEN
## The Church's View

*Systematic Theology,* Louis Berkhof, Banner of Truth Trust, 1941
*Evangelical Dictionary of Theology,* Marshall Pickering, 1984
*Pseudo-Dionysius, the Complete Works,* S.P.C.K., 1987

*Angels—Spirits Magnificent & Mighty*, Athanasius Recheis, 1976

*Tracts & Treatises*, Vol. 3, John Calvin, Berdmans Publishing Co., 1958

*Dictionary of the Christian Church*, Paternoster Press, 1974

*The Holy Angels*, Mother Alexandra, Minneapolis, 1987

*Caring Across the Seas*, Missions to Seamen

*The Unseen World of Angels & Demons*, Basilea Schlink, Lakeland, 1985

# CHAPTER SIXTEEN
## Conclusion

*The Holy Angels*, S.J. Ashby, Church Union Church Literature Assoc., undated booklet

## OTHER BACKGROUND INFORMATION

*Angels—God's Secret Agents*, Billy Graham, Hodder & Stoughton, 1975

*When Angels Appear*, Hope Macdonald, Zondervan Publishing House, 1982

*Angels, Angels, Angels*, Landrum P. Leavell, Broadman Press, 1973

*The Vision of Dorothy Kerin*, Morris Maddocks, Hodder & Stoughton, 1991

*Angels & Men*, Ladislaus Boros, Search Press, 1974

*Angels*, Charles & Annette Capps, Harrison House, 1984

*Angels Watching Over Me*, Betty Malz, Hodder & Stoughton, 1986

*Angels and Me,* Carolyn Nystrom, Moody Press,
    1978

*Send Me Your Guardian Angel,* Alessio Parente, Pa-
    dre Pio, 1984

*Angels, Elect & Evil,* C. Fred Dickason, Moody
    Press, Chicago, 1975

Booklets on angels accompanying teaching tapes
    from Radio Bible Class, Grand Rapids, Michigan


*The Illustrated Bible Dictionary,* Inter-Varsity Press,
    1980

*The History of Christianity,* A Lion Handbook, 1977

# Amazing and Inspiring True Stories of Divine Intervention

*They are with us always...*

**ANGELS**  72331-X/$4.99 US
  by Hope Price

**ANGELS AMONG US**  77377-5/$4.99 US/$5.99 Can
  by Don Fearheiley

*They happen when you least expect them
and need them most...*

**MIRACLES**  77652-9/$4.99 US/$5.99 Can
  by Don Fearheiley

# AMERICA'S MOST INSPIRATIONAL AUTHOR

## BEYOND OUR SELVES
72202-X / $8.00 US/ $10.00 Can

## TO LIVE AGAIN
72236-4/ $8.00 US/ $10.00 Can

## A MAN CALLED PETER
72204-6/ $8.00 US/ $10.00 Can

## SOMETHING MORE
72203-8/ $8.00 US/ $10.00 Can

## THE HELPER
72282-8/ $8.00 US/ $10.00 Can

## CATHERINE MARSHALL'S STORY BIBLE
69961-3/ $10.95 US/ $13.95 Can